Surrendered
—the sacred art

Shattering the Illusion of Control
and Falling into Grace
with Twelve-Step Spirituality

Turner Publishing Company
Nashville, Tennessee
www.turnerpublishing.com

Cover design: Maddie Cothren
Book design: Tim Holtz

Library of Congress Cataloging-in-Publication Data Available Upon Request

9781594736438   Paperback
9781684421923   Hardcover
9781684421930   eBook

Printed in the United States of America

To my grandson, Jack

Knowledge is better than ritual;
Meditation is better than knowledge;
Best of all is surrender
which brings with it peace.
—Bhagavad Gita 12.12

CONTENTS

Preface   vii

Living Surrendered, a Preview   xiii

Introduction   xv

PART ONE
WE ADMITTED WE WERE POWERLESS OVER OUR ADDICTION—THAT OUR LIVES HAD BECOME UNMANAGEABLE

Chapter 1   You Are the Problem   3

Chapter 2   I Gotta Be Me   9

Chapter 3   Stop Me'ing   16

Chapter 4   The Tao of You   25

Chapter 5   Being Powerless   34

Chapter 6   Yes, And   46

Chapter 7   Rock Bottom   52

PART TWO
WE CAME TO BELIEVE THAT A POWER GREATER THAN OURSELVES COULD RESTORE OUR SANITY

Chapter 8   Came to Believe   61

Chapter 9   A Power Greater than Ourselves   67

Chapter 10   Glimpsing the Unglimpseable   73

Chapter 11   Purpose   78

Chapter 12   Beyond Happiness   83

PART THREE
WE MADE THE DECISION TO TURN OUR WILL AND OUR LIVES
OVER TO THE CARE OF GOD AS WE UNDERSTOOD HIM

Chapter 13   God as We Understood God   93

Chapter 14   The Eternal Tao   104

Chapter 15   Your Will, Your Life   114

Chapter 16   Being Nobody   123

Chapter 17   God's Care, God's Grace   130

Chapter 18   Letting Go of Deciding   139

Chapter 19   Living Surrendered   144

PART FOUR
THE SURRENDERED LIFE

Chapter 20   Serenity   151

Chapter 21   Freedom of Imperfection   155

Chapter 22   Inner Seeing   163

Chapter 23   Forgiveness   171

Chapter 24   Humility   184

Conclusion   There Is Nothing You Can Do,
              and Only You Can Do It   192

Invitations   201

              Monk Begging for Food   202
              Just Sitting   203
              Passage Meditation   204
              Neti-Neti   205
              Third-Step Prayer   206
              Who Is This Aliveness I Am?   207
              Ensō   209

Acknowledgments   211

Notes   213

Suggestions for Further Reading   221

About the Author   223

PREFACE

The Indian philosopher J. Krishnamurti is famous for saying "Truth is a pathless land." The reason truth is pathless is that truth is here, now. It is reality, what the Taoists call the ten thousand joys and ten thousand sorrows of everyday life. You don't travel to find reality because you are already immersed in it. You need not travel to find truth either. All you must do is live the reality arising around and within you in each moment. And this again is why truth is pathless. No path can lead you to where you already are, therefore any path you take to "find truth" can only lead you away from it.

The same can be said of recovery. Let me explain. We tend to speak of recovery as a destination: a place we arrive at by following a path away from our addictions. Even the notion of the Twelve Steps, with which this book is intimately concerned, reinforces that idea: as if we might take a step, make a change, then another, and progress to a place where we are free of our addictions and their distorting, disfiguring influence, a place where our true selves will finally be recovered.

Nonsense.

There is nowhere you can go where you will not find yourself and all your complex yearnings, and no path you can take away from here and now. But this is not an invitation to despair. It is an affirmation of freedom emerging from the realization that there is nowhere to go, no one to be, and nothing to change, a freedom that comes with a radical acceptance of and being surrendered to what is.

This realization, this being surrendered, isn't under your control.

Surrender is not a matter of will but of grace; not a matter of *jiriki* (Japanese for "self-power") but *tariki* (Japanese for "other-power"). This is why I prefer to talk about being surrendered rather than surrendering. Surrendering is a willful choice to move from addiction to recovery, something I believe you cannot do. Being surrendered is being free from the false binary of addiction/recovery, being free from the fantasy that you may choose between them, and even from the fantasy that there is a "you" to do the choosing.

Which is why this isn't a self-help book but a self-helpless book. It is a book for the self exhausted by the effort to escape addiction, by the effort to follow a path from here and now to there and then, and by the effort to become a self instead of being Self. This book removes the illusion that any such path exists or that following it would be a good idea.

This book doesn't tell you how to get surrendered but rather points out that you already are surrendered, though you may be doing your best to deny and resist it. This book explores what is true when you are surrendered, and what it is like living surrendered, and does so in hopes that you will see that being surrendered is what is already so.

Don't read this book to be other than you are; read it and discover you are already other than you take yourself to be.

This is my second book on Twelve-Step spirituality, the first being *Recovery—The Sacred Art: The Twelve Steps as Spiritual Practice*. The previous book is the broader of the two, dealing as it does with a close reading of each of the Twelve Steps originally formulated by Bill W. This book is narrower in its focus, with its primary emphasis placed on the first three steps. You need not read *Recovery—The Sacred Art* to understand this book—each book operates independently of the other—but you may find that this book leads you to the other if you find yourself drawn to a broader and more inter-spiritual investigation into the theory and practice of Twelve-Step spirituality.

My concern in this book is with Steps One, Two, and Three:

1. We admitted we were powerless over alcohol—that our lives had become unmanageable.
2. Came to believe that a Power greater than ourselves could restore us to sanity.
3. Made a decision to turn our will and our lives over to the care of God as we understand God.

I focus on these steps not simply because they are central to the process of recovery but because they are the foundation of Twelve-Step spirituality. A deep understanding of the first three steps is essential if you are to recognize that what Bill Wilson and Dr. Bob Smith gave us in 1935 was not merely a way of engaging with alcoholism but a spiritual practice on par with any other.

My own reading of these steps widens their concern beyond alcoholism or any named addiction: you aren't merely powerless over this or that substance or behavior but over life itself. The discovery made possible with the first three steps is that not only can't you control your thoughts, feelings, and behavior, but you also can't control the thoughts, feelings, or behavior of anyone else either. Because control is impossible, your addiction to control is an exercise in a futility masked by addictive behaviors such as drinking, drugging, eating, and the rest. It's not that your life *has become* unmanageable, it's that life itself *is* unmanageable—so unmanageable, in fact, that you cannot even willfully turn your life over to God or any other higher power.

This understanding of the first steps is designed to make it unavoidably plain that you are not in control, and it is only when you have accepted this reality that you can learn to live without control. And so this is not a book about how to gain control through the Twelve Steps but how to live wisely and well without the need for control.

This book is written in a "stone-skimming" style. Think of each chapter as a flat stone skipping off the surface of a placid pond, and the space between paragraphs as the stone flying through the air before it makes contact with the pond to skip once more. While the laws of physics determine just where the stone will skim the water, there is no way for you or me to know exactly where that will be. This gives stone skimming and this book a somewhat improvisational feel.

As we shall see, improvisation is at the heart of what it is to be surrendered. As in improvisational theater, you have no control over the situation in which you find yourself. Your job isn't to control the situation or the other players but to say "yes, and" to whatever is happening around and with you. Saying "yes" is accepting the reality of what is so at this moment; saying "and" is your engagement with reality in a non-coercive manner, what the Chinese Taoists call *wei wu wei*. Saying "yes, and" is living the surrendered life.

Each paragraph is, in effect, my saying "yes, and" to whatever arose as this book emerged. There is a flow to this but not necessarily a logic. It doesn't *make* sense but rather skims off the sense that arises of its own accord. At first this wasn't a deliberate decision; it simply was the only way the book would be written. As I rewrote the text several times, I decided to keep the "stone-skimming" style, in part because I came to see it reflecting the surrendered life this book was exploring, but also because I feel that this style helps to create a sense of what the Japanese call *menju*.

According to Japanese novelist and philosopher Hiroyuki Itsuki, *menju* is the Japanese word for "face-to-face transmission." It evokes the image of two people sitting so close to each other "that they can hear each other breathing."[1] To my ear, *menju* is the best way to convey truths. While you and I cannot sit face-to-face, this book is written in such a way as to reach across the pages and approximate the intimacy and honesty of *menju*.

This style of writing lends itself to a bit of repetition. There are certain ideas that reoccur and bear repeating. Because this book seeks to approximate *menju*, face-to-face communication, I have allowed ideas to emerge and reemerge as they see fit, just as might happen if we were indeed speaking face-to-face. As one person put it during a Twelve-Step talk I was giving in Annapolis, "Repeating a truth over and again is the best way for some of us to at last recognize it as true. This isn't propaganda, it is persistence. Propaganda is the perpetuation of falsehood masquerading as truth. Persistence is the slow chipping away at our resistance to opening ourselves to truth."

Throughout this book are quotations from many different sources. When I quote from a book, I reference the source in the endnotes. When I quote from a sacred text, and use a published translation of that text, I again reference the source in the endnotes. Many of the translations, however, are my own, and these I do not reference. If there is no attribution assigned to any given translation of a sacred text, you should assume the translation is my own. Knowing this, you may wish to consult other versions to see where and how I have put my own spin on the original. In addition to citations from sacred texts from a variety of religious traditions, I also rely on concepts, most of them borrowed by Chinese and Japanese civilizations, which, like the notion of *menju*, may be new to you. While I do my best to convey the meaning of these words each time I use them, I have also added a glossary at the end of the book where I list and define each of these words.

As with my previous Twelve-Step book, I have made extensive use of conversations I had with dozens of people in various Twelve-Step programs. These conversations were not recorded, only written up by me after they happened. They are, by necessity, reconstructions. One criticism of my previous book was that while I went to great pains to mask the people I quoted, there was a sense that using names at all was somehow "outing" people. In this book I have removed almost all references to the people I quote and let what they said stand on its own without any reference to who said it. When knowing a bit about the speaker makes for a clearer understanding of what they said and why they may have said it, I have given you that information. The major exception to this regards my first sponsor, Burt. Burt has been an important part of my life for almost eighteen years, and while his recent death precludes our meeting and speaking, his words and wisdom continue to guide my life and inform this book.

LIVING SURRENDERED, A PREVIEW

What is living surrendered?

Living surrendered is being genuine—feeling your feelings without hesitation, thinking your thoughts without reservation, and staying present to it all.

Living surrendered is awakening to truth, your essential nature, the good and the bad, and finding yourself at home with what is.

Living surrendered is having your arms opened wide enough to embrace everything, even as you cling to nothing.

Living surrendered is holding nothing back, abandoning your escape route, not looking for alternatives, not thinking things can be or should be other than they are in this moment.

Living surrendered is seeing without distortion or deception, and knowing that it is possible to have an unconditional relationship with this moment and this moment and this moment.

Living surrendered is stepping out of hiding and abandoning refuge in security and confirmation, in affirmations and fantasies.

Living surrendered is going beyond what is comfortable, safe, and secure.

Living surrendered is free. But it costs you everything.[1]

INTRODUCTION

"We alcoholics are men and women who have lost the ability to control our drinking. We know that no real alcoholic ever recovers control."[1] Have you *lost* control over alcohol, food, drugs, or any other named addiction or did you never have control in the first place? I'm a food addict. I've been a food addict since I was a kid. I never *lost* control over food because I never *had* control over food.

If you talk about having lost control, you imagine that you once had control and that you might have it again. As Bill W. tells us, "All of us felt at times that we were regaining control, but such intervals—usually brief—were inevitably followed by still less control, which led in time to pitiful and incomprehensible demoralization."[2] An addict is born, not made. You didn't choose to be an addict; you were predisposed to your addiction from birth.

"I was an alcoholic toddler. Not that I drank as a baby, or knew anything about alcohol as a kid, but as soon as I did—as soon as I had my first drink at twelve—I was hooked. I didn't ease my way into alcohol addiction, I simply triggered an addiction that was already there."

This book draws on the experience of people wrestling with one type of addiction or another—alcohol, drugs, food, sex, gambling, pornography—but it isn't about named addictions at all. This book is about the addiction to which almost every human being is prone: the addiction to playing God. Playing God—insisting we are in control or should be in control of our lives, and hence all life, since our lives are impacted upon by all other lives—is the root addiction of humankind. This is why Bill W. says, "First of all we had to quit playing God."[3] Playing God is playing at being in control. You want to be in control of your life; you have been told since childhood that you can and must take control of your life, but reality says otherwise. Reality shows you time and again that you have no control.

"It's like you're a little kid sitting in the back of car driving down a highway. You assume someone is driving, someone is in control. As you get older you lean forward into the front seat and discover no one is driving the car. It's just gravity or physics or nature that is pulling the car along. Eventually you manage to climb into the driver's seat and grab hold of the steering wheel and try to control the car, but you discover the steering wheel isn't connected to anything, and the brake and gas pedals aren't connected to anything, and the whole thing is an illusion, and you are just careening down the highway at the mercy of nature. No wonder I drank!"

Imagine what is necessary to take control of your life. You don't live in a vacuum; other lives are constantly impinging on your own. So to control your life you must control other lives as well—and not just the lives of people close to you but all lives, indeed all life in general. To control your life, you must be in control of the entire universe, and you're not. So you imagine a God that is. The God of your understanding, as AA puts it. But this God isn't really God. It's just you projecting yourself, projecting your need for control.

The problem is you don't have control. You never did. And since you lack control, so does your God. You may insist otherwise. You may say your God isn't you but rather the Creator and Judge of all the universe. But then you have a problem because even this God doesn't seem to be in control of what happens. Think about it. If God were in control, things would turn out the way God wants and, since this is the God of your understanding, the way you want them to turn out as well. But they don't. Now you have another problem: once you realize that your God isn't in control, you must explain why. This takes you into the realm of theology, wherein the fundamental challenge is to explain why it is that the God you imagine isn't doing the things you imagine God is supposed to do.

Now you are no longer just playing God but playing God's defense attorney as well. You have put yourself in the odd position of having to defend the God of your imagining to yourself. The best way to do this is to, first, never admit that God is the God of your imagining, and, second, blame yourself for not being worthy of your God's love.

You may start to wonder if this God hates you or is punishing you for some terrible failing. Maybe this God you created to stop you from drinking (for example) is now punishing you for drinking. You are so lost in the game of playing God that you no longer realize you are playing a game at all. That's why if the Twelve Steps are to help you, you must first stop playing God.

"Sobriety isn't a trait you achieve and master. It isn't a brass ring you can grasp. Sobriety isn't a thing at all, and hence cannot be achieved. Sobriety is your natural state, the state you are in at this and every moment. You don't arrive at sobriety. You realize you are sober, and you realize that when you stop insisting otherwise."

WORKING THE STEPS

It works if you work it. In recovery we say this all the time. The statement isn't false, it's just not true the way we imagine it to be true. If you are "working the steps" you are still in control, and you are holding out the hope that one day you will get sober or clean and stay there. But this very notion of a steady-state recovery is false. That's why we say we are recovering rather than we are recovered.

My sponsor, Burt, once asked me to draw a picture that illustrated my understanding of the Twelve Steps. I drew a primitive staircase with Step One at the bottom and Step Twelve at the top, and a stick-figure "me" climbing from One to Twelve. He shook his head and drew his own image. It was an endless stairway with landings every twelve steps. Step One was at the top, Step Twelve was the step before each landing, and each landing was followed by another Step One. He also drew a stick figure, but where mine was climbing up, his was tumbling down.

"Gravity is your friend here," Burt explained. "You start at Step One and then tumble down to Twelve. Then you pick yourself up and pitch your tent on the landing. You've made it. But over time—and it doesn't take much time—you fall off the landing onto the next Step One and then tumble down again to the next Step Twelve and the next landing. Every landing gives you the illusion of liberation, but every landing is followed by another tumble. That's just true; that's just how things are—not only for addicts but for everyone. Twelve-Step spirituality isn't about learning how to rise powerfully but how to fall gracefully."

Imagine trying to remove the negative pole from a bar magnet. It can't be done. No matter how many times you cut off the negative pole, it reappears in the remaining bar magnet. Why? A magnet is not a magnet without both poles. The negative pole goes with the positive pole, and neither can be separated from the other. Now label the negative pole "addiction" and the positive pole "sobriety." Try as hard as you can, you cannot have sobriety without addiction: the one goes with the other. The key isn't to free yourself from the addiction pole or to cling to the sobriety pole, but to realize you are the magnet: you contain both poles. You have an addictive element and a sober element, but you cannot be reduced to one or the other. Knowing you are both poles frees you from the endless battle to be only half of who you are.

What does it mean to accept the addictive pole of yourself as an inescapable part of yourself? It means you are free to stop fighting yourself. It means you are no longer at war with yourself. And when you are no longer at war with yourself you are at peace. Sure, you feel the call to addictive behavior and the call to sober behavior, but these no longer disturb your equanimity.

The recovering alcoholic, for example, who has been surrendered to equanimity doesn't drink. But her sobriety isn't the result of any effort on her part but simply the consequence of her equanimity. She is sober because she knows her true nature and not because she has defeated alcoholism.

I eat compulsively. If I am presented with a plate of gluten-free fudge brownies (I have celiac disease and must avoid gluten), I am suddenly thrust into the battle of a lifetime: to eat or not to eat. As I wrestle with my addiction and try to defeat it with the power of sobriety, I intensify both poles of my being: the sober saint and the addicted sinner battle it out like Dr. Jekyll and Mr. Hyde. Mr. Hyde always wins. Then the now martyred sober saint retreats into the hollows of despair as I begin a cycle of self-loathing that almost always leads to more overeating. But, as odd as it may sound, when I realize that I contain both Dr. Jekyll and Mr. Hyde, I can simply walk away from their struggle. I don't eat the brownies, and I don't win. There is no winning or losing in this context. Having been surrendered to the truth of who I am, I no longer put energy into either pole and simply move on to what's next.

Why is ceasing to play God an essential precursor to the Twelve Steps? Because the Twelve Steps focus on your addiction, and your addiction arises from your desperate need to play God, to maintain the illusion of control. We like to think of addiction as a disease, but if the ultimate addiction is addiction to control, then the disease isn't alcoholism, compulsive eating, or opioid dependence but the disease of playing God.

If addiction is a disease, the disease is being you, the you that is both Dr. Jekyll and Mr. Hyde, the you that wrestles with yourself in an endless and futile battle for control. The cure lies with the ending of you, and the ending of you is the gift that arises from being surrendered.

THE ART OF LOSING

"We perceive that only through utter defeat are we able to take our first steps toward liberation and strength."[4] Surrender is an art, but not one you can master. Indeed, the very notion of mastery makes surrender impossible: you can no more surrender yourself than you can, as Zen philosopher Alan Watts used to say, bite your own teeth or hear your own ear.

While it is true that you cannot surrender yourself—you must be surrendered by a power greater than yourself—it is also true that you can struggle mightily to avoid being surrendered. Most of what you do to surrender is a subtle way to avoid being surrendered. Trying to surrender is like trying to be spontaneous. It can't be done.

Surely you are sincere when you admit you are powerless over your addiction, and that your life has become unmanageable (Step One), but then you go right on trying to manage your life by imagining a higher power that can save you from yourself (Step Two) and then willfully turning your will and your life over to the care of God as you understand God (Step Three) in order to secure that salvation. But you cannot willfully turn your will over to God because the will you intend to surrender is the will you need to do the surrendering, and the God to whom you wish to surrender is the God of your understanding, that is to say a projection of the very you that is the problem in the first place.

You cannot surrender, but you can be surrendered. You can discover that your life is unmanageable and hence beyond your capacity to surrender. When you do—when you know this is true the way you know your thumb hurts when you accidentally smash it with a hammer—you quit playing God; you simply quit. You don't decide to quit, plan to quit, or move toward quitting: you simply discover you are quit, and the only thing to do when you are quit is to live without managing things—to live surrendered.

"I haven't had a drink in ten years, but I don't take any credit for this. I don't think I had anything to do with it. In fact, if it were up to me, I'd still be drinking. For me not drinking isn't a choice—you know, to drink or not to drink—any more than taking cyanide is a choice. I know it sounds paradoxical but I now believe that neither my drinking nor my recovery was a choice. When I saw things through the eyes of my ego, I drank. When I saw that I was seeing things through the eyes of ego—which means

I was seeing them through other eyes—I simply saw what
was true and never drank again."

Whenever you realize the unmanageability of life—and
by "realize" I mean experience and know something so con-
cretely, so powerfully, that you cannot deny it in any way—
you are surrendered and healing happens. Realization of this
type comes when the "me" who is resisting the unmanageability of life is shattered or crushed—at least for a moment—by
the unmanageability of life. This happens only when you've
exhausted all the ways you can imagine resisting. You "win"
only after you've completely "lost."

This is what Jesus meant when he said, "Those who cling
to their life will lose it, and those who lose their life for my
sake will find it" (Matthew 10:39). The life you cling to is the
life you imagine when you succumb to the illusion of control
and manageability. Every time you cling to such a life you lose
it. Why? Because it isn't real: it's an illusion, a fantasy, a fiction of your own devising. But when you lose this illusory life,
you find true life, the surrendered life, and find yourself gifted
with the qualities of surrendered living: serenity, freedom,
gratitude, humility, and forgiveness, qualities we will explore
in part 4 of this book.

Years ago, Father Thomas Keating, one of the founders of
the Christian centering prayer movement, and a dear friend
and teacher since 1984, sat next to me on an interfaith clergy
panel in Texas. Someone asked him, "Are the death and resurrection of Jesus Christ essential to everyone's salvation?"
The speaker hoped to force Father Thomas into affirming
the Catholic teaching *extra Ecclesiam nulla salus*: "There is no
salvation outside the Church," and thereby lose his interfaith
street cred. After all, if Jesus's death and resurrection are
essential components of everyone's salvation, those religions

that lack these components cannot offer salvation. Seeing that he was struggling to find a way around this exclusivist teaching, I asked if I might answer the question. He agreed and I said, "The death and resurrection of Jesus Christ *are* essential to everyone's salvation; essential but not sufficient. Jesus shows you what must be done; now you have to do it for yourself."

Later that evening Father Thomas told me, "Crucifixion isn't something you can do for yourself. It isn't something you can do at all. Jesus was crucified by the Romans, not by himself. And he was resurrected by God, not by himself. Crucifixion is the act of being surrendered. Resurrection is the art of living surrendered. It all happens by grace rather than will. Being surrendered is the true gift of hitting rock bottom. Living a surrendered life is living as a perpetual novice, a beginner, and hitting rock bottom again and again. Being surrendered is a gift of fathomless love. Yet, while freely given, it costs you everything you have and think you are."

PART 1

We Admitted We Were Powerless Over Our Addiction—That Our Lives Had Become Unmanageable

CHAPTER 1

YOU ARE THE PROBLEM

According to the Buddhist monk and scholar Walpola Rahula, the Buddha taught that "the idea of self is an imaginary, false belief that has no corresponding reality, and it produces harmful thoughts of 'me' and 'mine,' selfish desire, craving, attachment, hatred, ill will, conceit, pride, egoism, and other defilement, impurities, and problems. It is the source of all the troubles in the world from personal conflicts to wars between nations. In short, to this false view can be traced all the evil of the world."[1]

The self or "me" you imagine yourself to be has two primary obsessions: permanence and control. It yearns for things to be permanent, steady state, and reliable. Since nothing is permanent, it strives to gain control over impermanence and bend it to its will—that is, to make it permanent.

"I did drugs out of desperation. I couldn't deal with the fact that everything around me was constantly changing. Life was chaotic; no, that's not it: life was chaos. But I thought it was only chaotic, that it could be something other than it was if I simply applied enough pressure. But there isn't enough pressure in all the world to change chaos into order. So if I couldn't make life the way I wanted it, I would escape from the way it was. I found my escape in drugs."

You are the product of conditions arising from both nature and nurture over which you have no control, and you find yourself arising moment to moment in situations over which you have no control. Your sense of continuity with the "me" arising in each situation results not from any permanent self that carries over from moment to moment but from the speed with which moments happen.

Your sense of "me" is an illusion not dissimilar from that produced by lights on a sign blinking on and off in a linear sequence and giving rise to the impression that the light is moving along the rim of the sign. The on/off blinking happens so quickly that your brain cannot recognize the "off" and focuses on the "on," giving you the illusion of a moving light rather than seeing this as it is: a series of static bulbs rapidly flipping on and off. The same is true of "me." "Me" arises moment to moment as part of situations that arise moment to moment. There is no "me" apart from these situations.

Burt, my first sponsor, used to say, "Just as you cannot separate heat from the sun or wet from the sea, so there is no you without the situation in which you find yourself."

You are happening in a greater happening, even as you insist you are independent of that happening. You can test this out for yourself: simply imagine yourself outside any situation. Be careful: don't imagine yourself floating in the vastness of empty space, for the vastness of empty space is still a situation. Imagine yourself alone without anything else around you, including space. You can't. "Me" is always situated somewhere, and since somewhere is always changing, the "me" that arises in it is always changing as well.

The fifth-century-BCE sage known to us as Ecclesiastes, the Teacher, speaks of the never-ending shifting of situations this way:

> *Everything in this world has its moment,*
> *A season of ripening and falling away.*
> *Moments of birthing and moments of dying;*
> *Moments of planting and moments of reaping.*
> *Moments of killing and moments of healing;*
> *Moments of demolition and moments of building.*
> *Moments of weeping and moments of laughing;*
> *Moments of mourning and moments of dancing.*
> *Moments of scattering stones and moments of*
>   *gathering stones;*
> *Moments of embracing and moments of releasing.*
> *Moments of tearing and moments of mending;*
> *Moments of silence and moments of talking.*
> *Moments of loving and moments of hating;*
> *Moments of warring and moments of peacemaking.*
> *What's the point of being willful,*
> *Demanding to reap that which has not yet grown?* [2]
>   (Ecclesiastes 3:1–9)

"Me" happens as part of each moment. "Me" ceases to happen with the cessation of each moment. Since you have no control over happening and ceasing to happen, you have no control over "me." And since this is too much to bear, "me" invents the story of you.

THE STORY OF YOU

Look at yourself in a mirror. Take a stack of sticky notes and write out the various versions of "me" you are: write one "me" on each sticky note. Place each note on your reflection in the mirror. When I do this, my notes say: "Rami," "Rabbi,"

"Husband," "Father," "Author," "Male," "Jew," "White," "Food Addict," and more. Eventually you will run out things to write about yourself. When you do, step back and see the "portrait of me" pasted on your reflection. Now step to the side of the mirror where you can no longer see your reflection. Now who are you? Who are you without a single note to define you? You don't know. You can't know because without labels and the stories that go with them, you're nobody at all.

You may object: "Not true. Even when I step away from the mirror, I'm still me." Fair enough, but who is this "me"? Without resorting to any label or story, who is the "me" you sense yourself you to be? You can't say, because there is nothing to say when there are no labels through which to say it. I'm not saying you cease to exist but rather without your story, the "me" you take yourself to be ceases to exist.

Step in front of the mirror again and notice that the "me" who is looking at the "me" in the mirror isn't the "you" in the mirror at all.

"I don't know if this makes sense, but when I say I'm a recovering drug addict I can't help wondering if that is really me. Not that I'm not recovering, or that I'm not addicted to heroin, but that, I don't know, but that I somehow feel like someone else. Almost like I'm playing an addict on TV, but it is reality TV."

"ME" IS A VERB

At the heart of the fiction of "me" is the notion that somewhere inside your body-mind is a thing, an entity that's called "me." So go hunting for it. Go as deep inside yourself as science allows and what do you find? Nothing. No "thing" at all. There is just life happening. Now ask yourself, "Who's looking?" Turn around and investigate the seer. Go as deep as you can and again what do you find? Nothing. No "thing" at all. And then ask, "Who is looking and finding nothing?" As you spin around and around looking for the looker, you will, by the grace of God, get so dizzy you topple over and, in the immediacy of falling, forget to keep looking.

"Koans make me dizzy," I once said to a Zen teacher deeply committed to both Buddhism and the Twelve Steps. "Yet still not dizzy enough," he replied. "When they make you so dizzy that you cannot maintain the illusion of 'you,' then you will fall to the ground and shatter. Like Humpty Dumpty, no one can put you together again." "Is that enlightenment?" I asked. "No," he said. "That's the moment before enlightenment. Enlightenment is the moment after, when a shattered Humpty-Dumpty just gets up and moves on."

"Me" isn't a thing but a management function. It isn't a piece of hardware but a piece of software. "Me" imagines it directs the play of your day; "me" provides the story that rationalizes and gives meaning to your various comings, goings, and doings. When the software is functioning as it should, your life runs smoothly enough. Not that there aren't moments of horror and tragedy, but "me" deals with them effectively and with the minimum amount of damage to itself and others. But the software can get corrupted. "Me" can get a virus that makes proper functioning more and more difficult. It picks up this virus from any number of sources—politics, religion, socialization—but regardless of where it comes from, the virus is always the same: "me" imagines itself apart from and at odds with the world around it. Rather than manage your personal life, "me" imagines it is in charge of all life. You imagine you are an emperor of life creating your own reality. Once you come to believe you are apart from the whole, you must dress the part. The clothes are gender, ethnicity, politics, nationality, religion—all the stickies you pasted on the mirror of self. But somewhere deep beneath the virus lurks the truth: the emperor has no clothes. Or more accurately, the clothes have no emperor.

"There is a moment when alcohol makes me feel like I'm king of the world—like Leonardo DiCaprio in *Titanic*. And then I take another drink and another drink and the ship goes down, taking me with it. Self-exaltation gives way to self-loathing. Maybe I drank to end the self, but there was no end, only endless degradation. The ending of self came with recovery. No, that's not it. It didn't come *with* recovery, it *was* recovery."

Without the trappings of "me" you awaken as the naked I'ing of all life. This I'ing—not a pronoun but a verb—is what the Hebrew Bible calls *Ehyeh*, the I'ing that is God (Exodus 3:14), the essence of all happening. Hindus call this *satchitananda*: pure being, pure consciousness, pure bliss.

Being free of "me," you realize this I'ing is you. You realize that, as the mythologist Joseph Campbell puts it, "the essence of oneself and the essence of the world . . . are one." And with that realization, Campbell explains, you are "free to wander as the essence of the world."[3]

CHAPTER 2

I GOTTA BE ME

In his early twentieth-century novel *A High Wind in Jamaica*, Richard Hughes uses the character of ten-year-old Emily Bas-Thornton to paint a vivid picture of what it is to discover "me":

> And then an event did occur, to Emily, of considerable importance. She suddenly realized who she was. . . . It suddenly flashed into her mind that she was *she*. . .
>
> She began to laugh, rather mockingly. "Well!" she thought, in effect: "Fancy you, of all people going and getting caught like this!—You can't get out of it now, not for a very long time: you'll have to go through with being a child, and growing up, and getting old, before you'll be quit of this mad prank!". . .
>
> Once fully convinced of this astonishing fact that she was now Emily Bas-Thornton . . . she began seriously to reckon its implications.[1]

To reckon with its implications, we must parse this text carefully. The event revealed here occurred *to* Emily; Emily didn't make it happen. Rather Emily was the happening itself. There was no Emily prior to this event. Yes, there was a little girl, and, yes, she most likely responded to the name "Emily" when called. But there was no sense of self; no "me"; no Emily as an object of cognition; no Emily per se. As Hughes puts it, "How could Emily have gone on being Emily for ten years without once noting this apparently obvious fact?"[2] What happened to Emily is that she shifted from an amorphous and undefined I'ing to a concrete and completely defined "me."

You don't decide to become "me," you simply discover that you are "me." Once you do, there is no escape from it. You're caught in the prank of "me" for a very long time. But who is caught? Was Emily caught as "me" or was the "me" caught as Emily?

Emily and her sense of self, her sense of being "me," arose together. Prior to that moment of arising there was a little girl whom others called "Emily" and who responded to that call the way a dog might respond when its name is called, but there was no inner calling, no inner naming, no inner owning of or identifying with the name. There was no sense of "me" separate from a larger sense of reality. Before the "me" that was Emily was the I'ing that is everybody in general and nobody in particular.

"There is nothing static or fixed in the universe," Burt would constantly remind me, "not even the universe itself. Everything is a happening, a verb rather than a noun. Because you get hung up on nouns, you imagine a world of fixed objects that you can possess and control. Because you get hung up on pronouns you imagine yourself the same way. But there are no nouns or pronouns, only verbs, only happenings, only change and flow and surprise. That's why it is truer to speak of I'ing than I. When you speak of I, me, and mine you are addicted to control. When you yield to I'ing there is only the liberation of being surrendered to what is happening."

I'ing is the subjective knower that cannot be known. I'ing is like an infinite ocean eternally waving. Each wave is a unique and temporary manifesting of I'ing. You are one of these waves, the one you call "me." As long as you know that "me" is a temporary manifesting of I'ing, things go smoothly. But when you imagine that the wave is other than the ocean, that "me" is separate from I'ing and hence from every other "me," then things go terribly wrong.

THE WORLD OF ME

The more you identify with "me" rather than the undefined and undefinable I'ing that is your truer self (or Self, if you prefer), the more you limit yourself to nothing but a growing pile of identifiers—those sticky notes. The more you identify as this "me," the more you are forced to defend this "me" against the larger world in which it resides. To maintain your sense of "me" you must control the world around "me," the world that impacts on "me," the world that threatens to topple the pile of sticky notes that is "me." This need to control alienates and isolates "me" even more, which makes the drive to control even stronger. The prank of "me" leads to playing God, and playing God leads to addictions of all kinds. Which brings us to the implications and consequences of being "me."

The primary consequence of being "me" is a conflation of I'ing with "me" and "mine." Your sense of being the undefined and undefinable I'ing is lost, and you are trapped in the myriad labels, stories, fantasies, and objects that define you as "me."

Let's look at this from another angle and see if it doesn't clarify things a bit. When you say "Here I am," the "I" that is here is the physical "you" that occupies a specific place that is the "here" at the moment you say "Here I am." Saying "Here I am" identifies the "I" with the body. But is this true? Are you that body?

While this "I" appears physically bound by the physical you, it can't really be you at all. For example, if you gain twenty pounds or lose twenty pounds, the "I" doesn't get fatter or thinner. Similarly, if you add ten years to the age you are now and imagine yourself saying "I" as this older you, you won't be imagining a different you but rather the "you" you now projected out to the "you" you will be then. And what shall you make of the biological fact that almost every cell in your body dies and is replaced every seven years, and yet you still claim to be the "you" you were seven years ago? You aren't your body.

"In OA we don't focus on weight per se, but the truth is I was very fat, obese really. Working the steps, the weight began to fall off, and I remember a moment—this was deep into my recovery—when I caught a glimpse of myself in a mirror, and said, "Oh my God, I was in that fat body all along. But then another thought came to me, if I lost even more weight I could still say that, and if I lost too much weight I could still say that. It occurred to me that no matter how skinny or even emaciated I got I could still imagine a thinner me inside. Then I realized that there is no me at all, only this imagining."

If your "I" isn't physical, perhaps it's psychological. When you were ten years old, did you think and feel the same way you do today? When you are eighty-five or ninety years old, will you think and feel the same way you do today? Probably not, yet you will continue to call yourself "I." So if you aren't the same physically, intellectually, or emotionally, what is the same? What is the "I" that is present as "I" throughout your entire lifetime? The story of "me."

"I often have the sense that I've been dropped into a stage play, given a name, a backstory, other people with whom to interact, and a situation—in my case, opioid addiction—in which to play out my part. I'm caught up in this play, this story. What I'm looking for isn't simply a way out of my addiction but a way out of my story."

OVERCOMING THE ME DELUSION

You are nothing without your story. The "prank," as Emily calls it, is not only the "me" caught in the story but also the story itself.

This might not be a problem if you were simply absorbed in the story, but you're not. There is always a sense of distance, separation, even alienation. Why? Because you have a nagging sense that the "me" lodged inside your head isn't really you at all. This is what Albert Einstein called humanity's "optical delusion." Overcoming this delusion, according to Einstein, is the real purpose of true religion and spirituality:

> A human being is a part of the whole, called by us "Universe," a part limited in time and space. He experiences himself, his thoughts and feeling as something separate from the rest—a kind of optical delusion of his consciousness. The striving to free oneself from this delusion is the one issue of true religion. Not to nourish it but to try to overcome it is the way to reach the attainable measure of peace of mind.[3]

While many Christians speak of original sin, I prefer to speak of original delusion: the delusion that the "you" you call "me" is separate from the world. Because you feel separate from the world you find yourself seeking to control the world.

But you are not separate from the world, and you cannot in anyway control the world, so you mask your failure and the existential horror that you are a failure behind one addiction or another. Your addiction isn't your central problem, your sense of a separate "me" is your central problem.

"This is the great double-bind," Burt would remind me periodically. "Your addiction is rooted in a fiction, the story of 'me.' That's why you can't overcome it, control it, recover from it once and for all: it isn't real. 'It' isn't a concrete thing you can master but rather a story you tell about who you are. Twelve-Step spirituality is a process of freeing you from that story and the 'me' who is its protagonist. Even your higher power is a character in your story. As your story drops away, 'me' and your higher power drop away as well. When this happens, you give up on the Twelve Steps and at last give in to them; you give up on recovery and give in to recovering."

Emily knew she would be "Emily" through childhood, adulthood, and old age, but she also knew there would be a time when "you'll be quit of this mad prank!" Most of us, once we get comfortable with the prank, are in no hurry to see it end. Indeed, we imagine lives after death—either reincarnated lives here on earth or ongoing lives on heavenly or hellish planes. Because it is hard to imagine a "me" that is not lodged somewhere in particular to maintain its sense of being someone in particular, we imagine new bodies not unlike the old bodies we will leave behind at death. These bodies may be physical or spiritual, but they are always somebody that is identifiably "me."

I suggest that neither Emily (or rather Richard Hughes) nor Einstein is talking about souls and an afterlife. Rather they are talking about the possibility of dropping one's story and with it the "me," and awakening as I'ing happening as everyone, everywhere, all the time. Einstein called this the "one issue of true religion." We can grasp his definition of true religion by reversing his statement. If the one issue of true religion is freeing oneself from the delusion of separate selfhood—"me"—then a true religion is one that makes this liberation its primary concern.

"Let's be crystal clear. The purpose of any particular religion isn't salvation or enlightenment but the perpetuation of that particular religion. That's why you don't stop being a Lutheran or a Catholic or Mormon or a Muslim or a Jew when you die. If getting free of my addiction means getting free from my story, and religion is an essential part of that story, I certainly can't turn to my religion for that. My religion doesn't want me to be free. It wants me to be a better Lutheran. In fact, it doesn't even want me to be saved unless being saved means being saved as a better Lutheran."

True religion seeks to free you from "me." Twelve-Step spirituality, as I understand it, is a "true religion" in that its sole purpose is to free you from "me" and in this way to free you from the addictions in which "me" is trapped. Is this possible? I think it is. Can you do it? I'm certain you can't. Liberation is an act of grace arising from profound surrender of self and story, something you cannot do for yourself—because, of course, you don't exist.

CHAPTER 3

STOP ME'ING

Think of a time when you were so engaged in something that all thought of "me" vanished. It could happen in any number of settings: watching a movie, listening to music, reading a book, walking in nature, writing, making love, talking intimately with a friend, or observing a toddler at play, for example. While there is no "me" present in these moments, there is activity—something is happening that is so all-encompassing that there is no room for a separate "me" to critique what is happening. This is a state beyond any sense of "me." Hindus call this *satchitananda*: pure being, pure consciousness, and pure bliss. *Pure* in this context means selfless, empty of "me."

Such moments happen of themselves and end of themselves. You are gone, and then you return. Yet things are not exactly as they were. Or rather, the "me" who returns is not exactly the "me" who disappeared. You are somehow more open, spacious, less attached to thoughts, feelings, desires, and cravings than you were prior to your disappearance. The thoughts, feelings, desires, and cravings may be no less, but your attachment to them is less. This is how you know that something happened in your absence.

Reb Nachman of Breslov (1772–1810), the great grandson of the Baal Shem Tov, the founder of Hasidic Judaism, called this *reshimu*, meaning "residue" or "leftover." In this case it refers to what is left of the me-less moment after "me" returns. Imagine purchasing a small bottle of expensive perfume, removing the stopper and setting the open bottle on a tabletop. Over time the perfume will evaporate, but the fragrance permeating the bottle and the surrounding air proves that perfume was there. Think of *reshimu* as the fragrance of the me-less moment that happened in the absence of "me." It is sensed in the body as softness, in the heart as compassion, in the mind as spaciousness, and in the spirit as radical hospitality welcoming whatever comes next without fear or resistance.

"I used to resent calling myself a 'recovering alcoholic.' I mean, how many years of sober living are necessary before I can call myself a 'recovered alcoholic'? But at some point I realized that as long as there is me, there is the fact of my addiction; as long as there is me, there is the possibility, no matter how slim I may imagine it to be, that I will start drinking again. Alcoholism and I go together. But I no longer despair over this pairing of alcoholism and me because I know that this thing I call 'me' isn't me at all, or at least not all of me. What this greater me is I can't say, but this greater something is a fact. Because I coexist with this greater something my alcoholism coexists with my recovery. And that is how I made peace with calling myself a recovering alcoholic rather than a recovered one."

THE CONFLICT OF OTHER THAN

Burt called me at home one night and said, "If you want to stop overeating, you must stop *me'ing*. But you can't change, and that's the good news! If you can't change, there is no need to bother trying to change. And when you stop trying to change, when you at last stop trying to be other than you are, you will discover that you are always other than you are. Do you understand what I'm saying to you? No? Good! Now we're getting somewhere!"

The more you seek to know yourself, the more conflicted things become. Knowing yourself requires you to be other than the self you wish to know. But you cannot be other than you are. You are the self you wish to know, control, and change. When you imagine otherwise, the conflict increases.

This conflict arises from your insistence that you are other than "me," when the truth is you are more than "me." You are "me," and there is nothing that can be done about that. You are also the I'ing that includes and transcends "me" the way the ocean includes and transcends its waves. When you seek to surrender yourself, you place yourself in conflict with yourself as "me" seeks to surrender "me" to a higher power which, as we shall see, is nothing more than a more subtle projection of "me." But when you awaken as I'ing, "me" is surrendered and the conflict ends.

THE TRAP OF HAVING

In Judaism, "me," the conflict-producing self, is called *mochin d'katnut*, narrow mind. The I'ing beyond conflict is called *mochin d'gadlut*, spacious mind. Narrow mind forever rummages through thoughts, fantasies, memories, labels, and stories to create the sticky note me. Spacious mind includes and transcends narrow mind: while it is aware of the portrait of me, it doesn't for one moment imagine that it is that portrait.

Narrow mind is all about having. Spacious mind is only about being. Having and being are described by the psychologist and philosopher Erich Fromm as "two different kinds of

orientation toward self and the world."[1] When operating out
of the having mode, your life is all about consumption, own-
ership, power, and control. When operating out of the being
mode, your life is all about relating, coexisting, being a part of
rather than apart from. This is spacious mind, the I'ing that
knows itself to be one with all as all the way an ocean is one
with its waves, and water is one with both.

Consuming is central to having, to living as "me." Consuming is one way to relieve the anxiety of being apart from the
whole of life, but its relief is temporary. As Fromm explains,
"Previous consumption soon loses its satisfactory character,"
and you find yourself needing to consume more and more.
"Me" defines itself by "the formula *I am = what I have and
what I consume*."[2] But you can never consume enough.

> "Some people eat to live and some people live to eat,
> but for me it was otherwise; for me eating was living. It
> got to the point where if I wasn't eating I feared I wasn't
> living, I was dying. It was as if chewing and swallowing
> replaced breathing as the central fact of my existence.
> You know that saying 'you are what you eat'? For me
> it was 'you are because you eat.' I couldn't stop eating
> because I didn't want to stop living. Eating was my way
> to immortality."

Narrow mind is the "me" trapped in endless having, in
endless consumption, and in an endless quest for power and
control that often falls into addictive behaviors that feed the
drama of "me" and narrow mind. Spacious mind has no
quest, seeks no power, and realizes the illusory nature of control. Narrow mind is a wave insisting it is the entirety of the
ocean. Spacious mind is the ocean knowing it is greater than
the sum of its waves.

Both minds are natural and necessary, but only narrow mind is prone to conflict and addiction. Narrow mind knows no limits; it seeks to expand the power of "me" as far as it can. Spacious mind has no limits and is therefore free from the need to expand at all. Knowing no limits, narrow mind seeks to overpower and gain control over others. Having no limits, spacious mind is unconcerned with competing "me's" and simply navigates what is rather than ceaselessly and compulsively trying to control it.

Once narrow mind sees that control leads to conflict, and conflict leads to addiction, and addiction leads to needless and often terrible suffering, it seeks to surrender. Spacious mind is already and always surrendered. The higher power to which narrow mind turns is the God of its own understanding, that is to say, a more subtle projection of itself. The higher power to which spacious mind is always surrendered is the God beyond understanding. Where narrow mind seeks to surrender to a Greater Me, spacious mind is surrendered to the absolute I'ing. Narrow mind wants to know what to do in order to free itself from itself. Spacious mind simply attends to what is.

"Before I got into Program I went to my pastor for help with my drinking. She told me all I had to do was believe in God and ask for his help. She then proceeded to tell me what and who God is. When I first entered AA, my sponsor told me all I had to do was believe in a higher power and turn my life over to him. Then he proceeded to tell me what and who this higher power is. After a while I realized that they were both wrong. God was the God of my understanding and I could tell myself what and who God is. As it turned out, I discovered that I had no more idea as to what and who God is than my pastor or sponsor, and that all God ideas were fantasies, projections. It isn't that God doesn't exist, only that any idea about God is simply a veil keeping me from God."

Because narrow mind is forever trying to be something it is not, it creates and situates itself in perpetual conflict. It experiences life, as the Buddha told us, as *dukkha*, unsatisfactory and steeped in suffering. Narrow mind's existence is a series of frustrations punctuated with transitory moments of happiness. If it simply accepted this as inescapable, narrow mind might find some relief in nihilism, but because it is embraced by spacious mind, it has intimations of something better than the life it lives. The mistake narrow mind makes is to imagine that this "something better" is actually "something more": more wealth, knowledge, power, and, most of all, more control. In its never-ending quest for more having and having more, "me" entraps itself in a world of lack. To mask its despair at not being able to overcome its sense of lack, it falls into the trap of addiction.

Spacious mind simply is, therefore it lacks nothing, desires nothing, quests after nothing. It is forever free. Where narrow mind wants to be anything but itself, spacious mind is content to be only itself. But remember, spacious mind includes narrow mind the way the ocean includes its waves. Spacious mind doesn't seek to end the waving of narrow mind or free narrow mind from the conflicts and addictions to which it is prone. Spacious mind simply sees what is as it is. Being surrendered is that seeing, and in that seeing is true liberation. The key isn't to erase "me" but to awaken as I'ing.

As the philosopher J. Krishnamurti tells us, I'ing "has nothing to do with acceptance, denial, and conviction. On the contrary, acceptance, denial, and conviction prevent understanding. To understand, surely, there must be a state of attention in which there is no sense of comparison or condemnation, no waiting for a future development of the thing we are talking about in order to agree or disagree."[3] This "state of attention" is spacious mind.

Narrow mind is conditioned by innumerable narratives: the sticky-note "me" comprised of the numerous traits, roles, beliefs, isms, and ideologies to which you subscribe. Spacious mind isn't unaware of all this but simply doesn't cling to any of it.

STEP BACK AND SEE

If this were a self-help book, you would expect to find the keys to achieving spacious mind and the liberation it promises. But this is not a self-help book, because the self is incapable of helping itself. You cannot put an end to this conflicted lesser self because trying to end it only adds to the conflict that feeds it. Nor can you put an end to conflict, for trying to do so is itself conflictual. You can only let it all be exactly as it is, and in so doing all effort to have it be what it is not ends. With the ending of effort comes the ending of conflict. The very desire not to be addicted feeds your addiction.

"I used to be at war with myself. My weapon of choice was food. There was the me I was warring with the me I wanted to be. When the me I wanted to be was winning, I ate to celebrate. When the me I was was winning, I ate to punish myself. As long as I played to win, I lost even when I won. It was only when I stopped playing that the war ended and with it all talk of winning and losing."

Your "me" must be surrendered, and when it is surrendered you discover there is no need to attain spacious mind because you are already spacious mind, and you need not seek liberation because you are already liberated. All you need is to see what is.

Burt once showed me photographs of paintings by Georges Seurat and Paul Signac, two artists who created in 1886 the style of painting called, at first mockingly, Pointillism. Rather than blend colors with brushstrokes as previous painters did, pointillists apply dots of color that only yield a picture when the viewer stands at a distance from the painting. Narrow mind looks at the painting and sees only the chaos of discrete dots. Spacious mind takes a broader perspective and sees both the dots and the greater picture. The "me" you take yourself to be sees itself as a dot on a cosmic canvas. Ignorant of the other points and the pattern they produce. "Me" imagines itself to be complete in and of itself. Unable to find any purpose to its existence, it takes refuge from the angst it suffers in drink, drugs, sex, gambling, food, and more. The key isn't to invent a story of "dothood" that promises salvation for each dot that subscribes to it but rather to become aware of the greater pattern of which each dot is a part. Being resigned, we surrender to the story of dot. Being surrendered, we awaken to the wonder of the painting. The former feeds us with faux meaning; the later awakens us to the intrinsic meaning of simply being a dot.

THE TRUTH OF HOPE

"When I listen to you talk about not being able to do anything," a young woman said to me at a recovery retreat I was leading, "I feel doomed. If I can't do anything to end my addictive cravings, if I can't do anything—even work the steps—I have no hope. How can you leave me without hope?"

Hope is always in the future. Hope is that someday you will be other than the "me" you think you are. Hope is that if you do this or that—work the steps or some other system—you can in time be other than who you are now. My suggestion is that you are already other than you think you are because who you think you are is never who you really are. When you are surrendered of all hope, you are surrendered of all thoughts of being other than you think you are. You discover that you are already free. Hope is irrelevant.

"Time is a distraction," Burt said. "It excuses inaction. As long as you imagine past, present, and future, you can excuse not being surrendered now by hoping for surrender in the future. Hope is the way you mask inactivity. 'Oh, I will be surrendered eventually. I just have a few more steps to follow and things to do, and then I will find what I seek.' Nonsense. You are what you seek, and seeking is counterproductive. Hope is the way you pretend you are making progress when in fact there is no progress to be made. Just wake up!"

Speaking this way is difficult because the very nature of language places you in the context of subject/object—the "me" you are and the "me" you want to be—and in the context of time—past, present, and future. Even when you talk about being in the now or being present, the very now you are talking about is of the past, and the present you hope to embody is of the future. This is not the fault of the ideas themselves but of the medium you are forced to use to investigate them. So don't fault the ideas until you've tested them in your own life. And give language a break, knowing that it is doing the best it can: using words to point to a reality beyond words. Think of words as the dots on a pointillist canvas, and step back from them to see the message they reveal.

CHAPTER 4

THE TAO OF YOU

Tao is the way things are and also the things themselves.
You cannot separate something from the way that something is. If you could extract the Tao of apple-ing from the
apple itself, it would no longer be an apple. In fact, it wouldn't
be anything. There is no apple without apple-ing.

What is true of an apple is true of you as well. There is no
"me" separate from the doing of you. The doing of you begins
at the quantum level and bubbles up through the atomic,
molecular, chemical, and cellular levels until it begins to happen on the psychological level that you call "me." For many
people, this is the end of the matter, but in fact the process
continues from the personal level to the interpersonal level to
the transpersonal level to the non-personal level of pure happening in which you disappear into the largeness of reality,
just as you once bubbled up from the smallness of reality.

There is only one dimension of "me" that matters to you:
the personal, psychological dimension. Of course, you care
about your physical health, but only because illness and death
impact the personal and psychological dimension. You may
care about the interpersonal dimension and your relationships
with loved ones both human and animal, but this concern,
too, is linked to the personal and psychological you. You want

a healthy body because when the body is well, you feel good. You want healthy relationships because when your relationships are loving, you feel loved. The problem isn't with the desire for health or love but with the illusion that health and love are steady-state phenomena: that you can be healthy and loved all the time, that you can control Tao.

"I loved the bottle more than I loved my husband. The bottle was more reliable. It was always there when I needed it and had no other desire than to serve me. My husband wasn't there to serve me and wanted me to serve him. I resented him and loved the bottle all the more. Then there came this moment—a moment of grace, I guess—when I realized the bottle was just like my husband: it wasn't serving me, I was serving it. That was the moment when I made arrangements to attend my first meeting. In the end I left them both."

In *The Tao of Sobriety*, authors David Gregson and Jay Efran explain that "central to the nature of addiction is the concept of control. Individuals who use alcohol or other drugs to control their feelings often succumb to the 'illusion of control'—that they now have the power either to avoid the 'low' of unpleasant experiences or to create a permanent 'high' to mask the boredom of everyday life events."[1]

Everyone wants to be in control. Because no one lives in isolation, because we are each connected to one another and to the greater unity from which all diversity comes, if we are to be in control we must be the boss of all reality. We must be God, assuming, of course, you imagine God to be the Boss.

To be free of the desire to be boss, you must see the true nature of things and understand the Tao not as an object of investigation but as the very nature of nature itself. To do this, you must go deep into things until there are no things at all but only the flow of Tao. Here there is no boss and no one to be bossed. Here there is just the wild flow of creativity itself. Addicts don't want to go with the flow; we want to control the flow.

THE WAY OF IMPERMANENCE

The Chinese word *tao* is often translated as "way," not in the sense of the "way to" but in the "way of." Tao is fluid, dynamic, and ever moving. Tao is the process of rising and falling, birthing and dying. As the poet and translator David Hinton describes it, Tao is "a generative cosmological process, an ontological pathway by which things come into existence, evolve through their lives, and then go out of existence, only to be transformed and reemerge in new form."[2]

Rather than try to describe Tao, we might point toward the reality of it via the iconography of the *taijitu*:

The simple message of the *taijitu* is the interconnectedness of all opposites represented by *taiji*, the teardrops of yin and yang (dark and bright) flowing into the other, and *wuji*, the circle of the absolute that embraces them both. The *taijitu* is neither monistic (*wuji* alone) nor dualistic (yin and yang alone), but non-dual, an all-encompassing reality that holds both the one and the many without being reduced to either.

Yin and yang go together; you can't understand the one without the other. The same is true of recovery: addiction and recovery go together and define one another. But the dance of addiction and recovery is played out in a larger field of awareness, the *wuji*. Taking refuge in the larger field doesn't do away with addiction or make recovery a permanent state but rather frees you from the delusion that you can, or what's worse, you must, do away with addiction and make recovery a permanent state.

The genius of the *taijitu* is that it frees you from having to free yourself. You are neither a saint ensnared in the sin of addiction nor a sinful addict striving to free yourself for sainthood. You are a sinning saint and a sainted sinner.

"This is dangerous talk, my friend," a well-beloved sponsor told me. "I never encourage people to accept their addiction as natural to themselves. I want them to struggle against addiction, not to excuse it."

I never argue about such things. Perhaps he's right. Perhaps I'm wrong. Perhaps something else entirely is true. What I might not say to him, however, I will say to you: fighting your addiction doesn't work. Being at war with what is creates endless conflict that, in my experience, is more apt to lead me deeper into my addiction than out of it. Being surrendered to reality doesn't surrender me to my addiction but to the greater *taijitu* that includes and transcends addiction. Opening to the truth of "me" allows you to see what is and allows your actions to arise out of what is rather than out of any fantasies about what is.

But do not mistake the truth of "me" for your truths. Your truths are merely ideas rooted in your understanding, which is rooted in "me" rather than reality. The truth of "me" is the simple fact that "me" is a construct, a narrative or series of narratives that defines you as "me." When you see the truth of "me," you see through "me" to the greater I'ing. When you see your truths, all you see is "me." When you see through "me," you see the truth.

THE REALITY OF CHAOS

As Hinton explains, "Vast and deep, everything and everywhere: existence is alive somehow—magically, mysteri-
ously, inexplicably alive. Nothing holds still."[3] To be present
in, with, and as Tao is to be present in, with, and as the arising
of this moment. To live in, with, and as Tao is to live with the
fluidity of things. To live with the fluidity of things is to live
the changing that is each moment. To live with changing is
to realize that your unchanging "me" is unnatural and funda-
mentally flawed.

"When I first entered Program I was gifted with having
my addiction lifted from me. I simply stopped using
drugs. Then I wondered why, if I wasn't doing drugs, I
still needed to attend meetings. So I stopped attending.
Then I started drugging again. I just couldn't figure out
if I was drug addict or a recovering drug addict. Then I
realized this wasn't a choice. I was both. And in time I
discovered I was neither as well."

The book of Genesis tells us about the fluidity of reality:
the earth is *tohu va vohu*, that is, wild, chaotic, empty of all
permanent form (Genesis 1:1). The first act of God—God as
Genesis 1 understands God—is to shed light on chaos and
then to call forth from the midst of chaos the seeming order
of the universe. What God doesn't do is slay chaos. Just under
the surface of reality as you experience it is *tohu va vohu*: an
astonishing emptiness, a fluidity from which all form arises
but does so only temporarily. We humans seek to order
this chaos, something even God doesn't do. Because we are
addicted to order and permanence, we are addicted to control,
and because order, permanence, or control are impossible to

achieve, we grow increasingly ill at ease with reality. As the philosopher Alan Watts explains:

> Indeed, this is the common attitude of man to so much that he loves. For the greater part of human activity is designed to make permanent those experiences and joys which are only lovable because they are changing. Music is a delight because it is rhythm and flow. Yet the moment you arrest the flow and prolong a note or chord beyond its time, the rhythm is destroyed. Because life is likewise a flowing process, change and death are its necessary parts. To work for their exclusion is to work against life."[4]

Ecclesiastes and the Taoists show us how to be at ease with reality; how to trust the Tao and surf the chaos. But trusting and surfing require you to be surrendered to *tohu va vohu*, to be stripped of any notion that you know what's happening or, worse, that you can control what's happening.

Reality, as the Taoists put it, is *tzu-jan*, "of-itself-so." Reality arises according to its own nature: when the conditions for something to happen ripen, that something happens no matter whether you like it or not. What makes you wise isn't your capacity to predict what is coming but to ride it out when it comes. What makes you foolish is your insistence that reality can be other than it is and your attempts to conform instead to what you want it to be.

Riding the wave of reality is what it is to be surrendered. Two key elements to successfully surfing on an actual surfboard are to keep a low center of gravity and to continually adjust your feet in response to the wave. For a seasoned surfer these actions are second nature, of-themselves-so. You don't seek to control the wave or the board, rather you allow the wave to tell you where to place your feet on the board. Moving in accord with reality is called *wei wu wei*, non-coercive or unforced action. The philosopher Aaron James calls this *adaptive attunement*. He writes, "Being adaptively attuned to a changing natural phenomenon, in part by not needing to control it, is at once a kind of freedom, self–transcendence, and happiness."[5]

GET OUT OF THE WAY

The Buddha rarely responded to metaphysical questions, preferring instead to focus his students on the practical work of liberation. To one questioner obsessed with metaphysical concerns the Buddha said, "Imagine you're struck by a poisoned arrow, and to save your life the doctor must remove the arrow immediately. You insist, however, that before the arrow is removed, you must know who shot it, his age, his parents, and why he shot it. What would happen? You'd die before getting your questions answered. Life is too short for endless metaphysical speculation that cannot in any case bring us closer to truth."[6] Let your speculation go and pull out the poison that is killing you.

Alan Watts taught, "The secret in Taoism is to get out of one's own way."[7] The secret to getting out of your own way is to realize that the "me" that is in your way isn't you at all. This "me" is the "me" of your understanding, a pale version of the God of your understanding, who seeks to empower itself by surrendering to the God of its understanding. Getting out of your own way isn't a willed act, a tactic for liberation, but rather the very nature of things when you are surrendered to reality as it is rather than as your imagined "me" pretends it is.

The world of your imagination is ordered by what the Taoists call *tsu*. *Tsu* is a fixed order, the order that you perceive when you measure or speculate about things. *Tsu* is valuable but not all-encompassing. There is a deeper order that is not imposed on reality but arises from the very nature of reality. The Taoists call this order *li*, the innate pattern of things in themselves. *Li* is the nature of nature naturing.

In the prologue to his gospel, John refers to the same idea as *li* calling it *Logos* ("order"): "In the beginning was Logos, the Logos was with God, and Logos was God. Logos was with God in the beginning. Through Logos all creation arises; without Logos nothing arises" (John 1:1–3). We find the same idea expressed some centuries earlier in the book of Proverbs where *Chochma* (*Sophia*, in Greek; *Wisdom*, in English) reveals herself as "the deep grain of creation, the subtle current of life" who existed before creation and through whom all creation comes (Proverbs 8:22–31). While reality in and of itself (*tzu-jan*) is wild and unfathomable (*tovu va vohu*), it also has its own innate wisdom, order, and grain (*Chochma*, *Logos*, *Li*). Being surrendered to reality is being surrendered not only to life's wildness but also to its wisdom, order, and grain.

As Watts explains, "The order of *li*, of the infinite complexity of organic pattern, is also the order of our own bodies, and of our brains and nervous systems. We actually live by that order."[8] Yet we continually impose *tsu*, the fixed order arising from our speculations *about* reality, on reality. The conflict between the order you desire, the order that comes from your desire to control the world around and within you, and the natural, organic order of things as they are, is the conflict that triggers your addiction.

"I sometimes call myself a narcoholic: I was addicted to sleep and used alcohol and pills to in a sense stay asleep even when I was outwardly awake. I was sleepwalking through my life because being awake in my life was too frightening."

This, I suggest, is what Jesus meant when, seeing his disciples asleep in the Garden of Gethsemane, he said, "The spirit is willing but the flesh is weak" (Matthew 26: 41). You are called to stay awake to reality, but when doing so becomes an effort of will, a struggle to overcome *tsu* (imposed order) and recover *li* (natural order), you always yield to sleep. But when you realize that *li* is already your truest nature, wakefulness is simply what happens of-itself-so. It is because you fail to realize the truth about reality that you nod in agreement with the apostle Paul when he says, "I don't understand why I do what I do. What I want to do, I don't do; what I don't want to do, I do" (Romans 7:15).

You get in your own way when you try to do what you are already naturally doing, and when you try to become who you already are. But you can't get out of your way until you see the true nature of things. When you see the true nature of things, you discover you are no longer in your way, so nothing needs to be done. When no thing needs to be done, you are living *wei wu wei*, effortlessly.

CHAPTER 5

BEING POWERLESS

Being surrendered is an act of grace. It arises of itself at the moment you realize you are truly powerless. As Father Thomas Keating writes, "To be powerless means to be absolutely helpless. In other words, you can't do anything under your own steam, willpower, or any amount of strategy. You're hooked. Overwhelmed, wiped out."[1]

When you are hooked, overwhelmed, and wiped out, the only thing you can do is cry for help. Your cry for help is not an act of free will; it isn't a strategy for avoiding desperation or triggering salvation but arises out of the very nature of your desperation.

Burt asked me, "Have you ever fallen off a ladder or down a flight of stairs? Have you ever been in a terrifying and dangerous situation over which you had absolutely no control? What did you do? You cried out! You didn't think about crying out. You didn't wonder if crying out would be of any help to you. You simply cried out; the cry simply erupted of its own accord. This is what it is to cry out from the depths of your addiction."

You cry out because there is nothing else you can do; it simply happens. Nothing happens until the conditions for it happening are present to such a degree that the thing that can happen must happen. When the conditions for rain are ripe, it rains. If the conditions are not yet ripe, it doesn't rain. It isn't that the conditions make rain happen; the conditions for rain and raining itself are the same. What is true of rain is true of recovery. It isn't that the condition of powerlessness and desperation give you the willpower to cry for help but that the condition of powerlessness and desperation itself cries for help.

Father Thomas and I were talking during a retreat. I asked him how he understood Jesus's teaching, "Ask and it will be given, seek and you will find, knock and the door will be open to you" (Matthew 7:7). "First let me tell you what it doesn't mean," he said to me. "It doesn't mean ask and in time God will answer you. It doesn't mean seek and over time you will find what you are seeking. It doesn't mean knock and wait, and in a moment or two the door will be opened for you. Translations that insert time into this teaching are missing the point of the teaching. What Jesus is saying is this: Asking is the answer, seeking is finding, knocking is opening. There is no time lag; it all happens of a piece in the moment."

The cry t hat erupts at the moment of absolute powerlessness shatters both the "me" that is playing God and the God it is playing. Keating writes, "We feel [the cry for help] from the very depths of our being. Something in us causes our whole being to cry out, 'Help!'"[2] And that cry itself shatters the game of addiction.

"Let me tell you the truth about addicts. Most of us don't want to recover. We just want to manage our addiction so we can continue to do whatever it is that is destroying our relationships and killing us without it in fact destroying our relationships and killing us. I wouldn't stop drinking if I could master alcohol. If there was a pill I could take

that would allow me to drink without becoming the
sick bastard I become, I'd take the pill and skip the
meetings."

The key to recovery isn't the knowledge that you have
an addiction, it is the realization that you are powerless and
your life is unmanageable. The "advantage" addicts have
over non-addicts is that their addictions make powerlessness and unmanageability inescapable and undeniable, while
non-addicts can limp along nursing the pretext of power and
control. Everyone is powerless; no one can manage life. Unless
and until you are forced to face this fact, the conditions are
never right for the desperate cry for help to spontaneously
arise from the depths of your being.

Surrender is a process; being surrendered is not. Surrender takes time; being surrendered happens in an instant.
Surrender is a tactic in which you engage to achieve a goal:
"to improve the quality of your life, reduce stress, and have
much more fun by lifting the curse of being overly serious,"as
Dr. Judith Orloff puts in *The Ecstasy of Surrender*.[3]

Surrender, as Dr. Orloff and so many others believe, is
a means to an end; being surrendered is the end in itself. To
be surrendered means everything is just as it was but you no
longer resist it.

"I expected that working the Twelve Steps would make
me fearless, but that was not the case at all. What I found
was that the fear was still there, but I was no longer afraid
of it."

"I think my drinking was my act of resistance. I mean, I
couldn't make things go my way, so I drank as a way of

saying 'F--- you' to the world. And if I'm honest, and I try to be, I didn't mind the drinking at all. I liked it. I liked blaming my problems on the world and saying 'F---- you' to the world. It made me feel like a hero. Like a resistance fighter, you know? What I didn't like was what I did when I drank, and how my drinking affected my family. Of course, that didn't stop me from drinking. Nothing stopped me from drinking; nothing I did, anyway. I just stopped drinking. I mean I didn't even turn my life over to my higher power—at least not intentionally. I simply slid into hell and Something pulled me through and out again. Was it God? Not the God I knew, not the God of my understanding. I don't know what it was, so I just call it Something."

REALITY WINS

Judith Orloff concludes her book *The Ecstasy of Surrender* this way: "Let's dare to surrender anything that stands between ourselves and our joy."[4] What stands between you and your joy is the "me" you imagine yourself to be. The problem is you can't surrender "me," for the "me" that must be surrendered is the "me" that is doing the surrendering. So what can you do? Leave joy alone and focus on reality instead.

When you focus your attention on reality you discover that there is nothing standing between you and reality. Even if you resist seeing what is real and take refuge in the delusions of "me," refusing to see what is real and taking refuge in "me" is still part of reality. When it comes to surrender, you can't win. When it comes to reality, you can't lose. It is all a matter of seeing clearly.

When you see life as both the ten thousand joys and the ten thousand sorrows, clinging to the former and warding off the latter ceases of its own accord. When you see "me" desperately clawing after joy, you cease to identify with the "me" that is seen and realize the I'ing that sees. When you see that "me" cannot surrender itself, all concern with surrender ends and you realize you have already been surrendered.

THE BONDAGE OF SELF

The *Big Book* puts it this way: "Relieve me of the bondage of self, that I may better do Thy will."[5] What is the bondage of self? It is every idea you have of who you are, who you should be, and what keeps you from being who you should be. The bondage of self is the "me" that pretends to be unbound.

"I came into program with the expectation of learning how to do God's will. I assumed God's will was that I stop boozing. But my sponsor said, 'Who do you think you are that you could possibly know what God's will is? Only God knows what God's will is. For all you know, God's will is that you drink yourself to death.' I started to cry. Literally. He ignored my sobs. 'Maybe joining AA is contrary to God's will,' he said. 'Maybe you don't need to stop drinking at all.' And you know what happened? I stopped drinking. Right then and there. In time I came to understand that drinking and not drinking were both acts of my will fighting against God's will. When I realized I had no frigging idea of God's will, I just stopped everything. Because I didn't know anything. And when I didn't know anything, I knew I no longer had to drink. Damn, I no longer wanted to drink. At the time I thought my sponsor was a jerk. In hindsight, I think he was a genius."

There are many methods to maintain the illusion of "me," and all them carry a degree of suffering intrinsic to the method itself. If you seek salvation in religion, you find yourself burdened with overcoming sin, karma, ignorance, or whatever your religion insists is at the root of your suffering. If you seek salvation in a bottle or a needle or in food, you find your life burdened by overcoming addiction. Whatever your method for maintaining "me," you find yourself at war with yourself. Whether you seek to surrender to the God as your religion imagines God, or to the God of your own imagining, you are still caught in the trap of surrendering rather than the liberation of being surrendered.

"Few of us really believe we are powerless. Sure, we admit that so far we haven't been able to free ourselves from the demons of our addictions, but just beneath all our surface talk about surrendering to our higher power is the addict employing surrender as a tactic and thus continuing the delusion of control."

When surrender is a tactic, it is just another means of control, another effort to impose your will on your disease. Surrender is beyond your power. If it weren't, you would have no need of a higher power. The genius of Twelve-Step spirituality isn't that it teaches you to surrender but that it exhausts you in the effort to surrender so that at last you surrender surrendering, and find yourself surrendered.

"I try to surrender, I do. I try and try and try and try, but it never takes. I'm not saying I fall back into drugs, only that I know I'm fighting my addiction rather than allowing God to take it from me. I'd like to end the fight and surrender, but it seems I'm powerless to do so."

"The reason you can't change," Burt said, "is that you are always changing. In order for the ever-changing you to change, it would have to first become static, fixed, and steady state. If you are *X*, perhaps you can become *Y*. But if you are nothing in particular, how can you become something else? It is the static that is impossible, not the change."

The willed act of surrender is a way to preserve the notion of a fixed "me." Since the "me" that is to be surrendered is also the "me" that is doing the surrendering, nothing really changes and the illusory "me," the "me" of your imagination, remains. The more it seems to hang on, the more it allows for the illusion of being fixed and static, the more out of touch you are with reality. Nothing in reality is static. There are no nouns in the universe, only verbs. This is what the Bible tells you when it refers to God as YHVH, from the Hebrew verb *h-y-h*, "to be" or "to happen." This is what you fail to know when Bible translators render the dynamic YHVH as the static "Lord." As long as you imagine a Lord above with the power to free you, you cannot realize you are part of the divine Happening that is freedom itself.

"It is difficult for Westerners to realize that Brahman, God, is one's truest nature," Swami B. said. "They hear this and think the Atman or Self I am talking about is the ego, the self they imagine themselves to be; the self they see when they look in a mirror or the self they create when saying 'I am this, I do this, I like this.' Like any wise guru, Bill W., who would hate being called 'guru,' doesn't tell you who you are. He only allows you to discover who you are for yourself by inviting you to exhaust the God-playing self in the futile effort of surrender."

THE ADDICTION TO BEING FREE

Don't imagine you must end your addiction to be free. Instead, come to realize through your own experience that your addiction, your cravings, your desires, your suffering are simply part of the play of God, the play of Absolute Reality. Just as the sky isn't affected by the various clouds it carries, so you, once surrendered to Absolute Reality, are no longer affected by the suffering you carry. Everything is just as it is, and perhaps for the first time in your life, this is just fine.

The need for things to change ends when you realize that things are always changing. The need for things to be other then they are ends when you realize that things are always other than they were. Continuity is an illusion created by the narrow mind, the "me" craving permanence. When you see the truth of what is, you discover that what is is always morphing into what is next.

When you see things as they are, when you see your craving and your resistance to craving as necessary expressions of the conditions ripening at the moment, you realize that the one who sees both is attached to neither. This is the liberation toward which Twelve-Step spirituality points: not the ending of addiction or suffering or anything else for that matter but rather a spacious welcoming of everything without the need to exchange one state for another. When there is no exchange and only change, then there is liberation.

"That's why we speak of recovering rather than being recovered," Burt said. "Being recovered is a permanent state of non-addiction. But nothing is permanent. I know that while I may eat wisely today, I may not eat this way tomorrow. So I'm not recovered, I'm recovering. What am I recovering from? I'm not recovering from compulsive overeating; that is just the way my disease manifests. I'm recovering from my true addiction, the addiction to 'me,' and the addiction to control that 'me' requires. I'm recovering from my compulsive resistance to reality as it is and my addiction to the fantasy of reality as I so desperately want it to be."

"I entered program desperately hoping to be other
than I am. I was a pill addict and I wanted to be an ex-
pill addict. The best I could manage was becoming a
recovering pill addict, but still the noun that defined me
was 'pill addict.' I struggled to be this other me—this ex-
pill-addict me—for years, and then, without any effort on
my part at all, the struggle ceased. I just realized I wasn't
a pill addict or an ex-pill addict or a non-pill addict or
anything else. I just was, and that was enough."

The addiction under which almost all humans suffer is
the addiction to resisting what is. As J. Krishnamurti explains:
"The *what is* is what you are, not what you would like to be;
it isn't the ideal because the ideal is fictitious, but it is actually what you are doing, thinking, and feeling moment to
moment. *What is* is the actual, and to understand the actual
requires awareness, a very alert, swift mind."[6]

A swift mind is not a mind racing from one thing to another
but a mind that is aware of all things changing moment to
moment. This mind is aware of preferences but holds no preferences; it is aware of sanity and insanity but does not choose
between them. Free from the obligation to choose, it rests in the
flow of this and that even as it is free from this and that. Being
free from this and that doesn't allow you to choose sobriety but
simply eliminates the conditions that give rise to its opposite.

What you want is to be free from addiction. What you get
is freedom from the addiction to being free.

I AM NOT MYSELF

A fifty-something woman at a Twelve-Step retreat said to
me, "If I'm not who I think I am; if I'm not this 'me' you are

talking about, then I'm nothing at all. Is this what you are offering me: endless nothingness, being nobody? I want to be my best self, not some no-self."

What if your best self is no-self? What if as nothing you have room for everything? What if by not choosing to be this or that or the other, you are this and that and the other, and have the capacity to draw on anything and everything that allows you to embrace the ten thousand joys and ten thousand sorrows of your everyday life? What if? I'm not telling you this is what you will realize when you stop playing God and live the Twelve Steps; I am inviting you to find out by not playing God and living the Twelve Steps.

In the book of Genesis we read about the death of Sarah. "Sarah lived one hundred years and twenty years and seven years; these are the years of Sarah's life" (Genesis 23:1). While the English translation is clear, the Hebrew is ambivalent, allowing for a very different reading: "Sarah lived one hundred years and twenty years and seven years; these are the two lives of Sarah." Sarah is paradigmatic of all of us. We all live two lives. Life 1 consists of two phases: a longer phase (one hundred years) and a shorter phase (twenty years). Life 2 consists of one much shorter phase (seven years). Don't take the numbers literally. Simply understand them to mean "longer," "shorter," and "shorter still."

Life 1, Phase 1, is the stage of material having. You focus on getting things and owning things, and often measure your worth, value, and success by how many things you have managed to get and keep. But eventually you realize that no matter how much you have, you are still haunted by lack and insufficiency. The stress of having (and the accompanying anxiety of keeping what you have) has not resulted in the joy of being. You ask yourself, "Is this all there is?" Asking this question may cause you to redouble your efforts to have even more, or it may cause you to slip from Life 1, Phase 1, into Life 1, Phase 2.

Life 1, Phase 2, is the stage of spiritual having. You pursue the spiritual in the way you once pursued the material. You fill your home with spiritual books, collect *malas* and statues of gods and goddesses, amass mounds of smooth stones with meaningful words etched into them, go on retreat after retreat, attach yourself to gurus of every stripe, and subscribe to magazines that sell the spiritual just as you once subscribed to magazines that sell the material. You no longer crave having, you now crave being.

In time, and usually in less time than it took to reach the end of Life 1, Phase 1, you come to the end of Life 1, Phase 2. You've read all the books, chanted all the mantra, sat at the feet of so many gurus you no longer remember who said what, and the old question returns: "Is this all there is?" While you might hear in this question a challenge to find the next book, the next retreat, or the next guru, you might also hear that there is nothing more you can do. You are powerless. At that moment you are surrendered to what is just as it is.

No longer craving "authentic being," you simply are. This is Life 2. You may still read, meditate, chant, and go on retreat, but you no longer do so to get something but simply for the joy of doing these things. To know if you are in Life 2, ask yourself what motivates you to do what you do. If there is something you hope to achieve, you are still in Life 1. If what you do is done simply for the joy of doing it, you might be in Life 2.

"I thought sobriety was the great gift of working the steps. I was wrong. The great gift—or maybe the greater gift—is joy. Not the joy of sobriety but the joy of simply being joyous, effortlessly joyous, gracefully joyous."

Life 2 is being surrendered to reality. You still have the same feelings, the same likes and dislikes as before, but you no longer struggle against them or yield to them. As Father Thomas Keating explains, "It is not a question of overcoming all our particular feelings but acknowledging and recognizing that we have these feelings without identifying ourselves with them. . . [We] face the truth of our feelings without identifying with them, acting them out, or objectifying them and blaming them on other people."[7]

Facing the truth of our feelings without being attached to the "me" that identifies with those feelings, you act for the flourishing of all at the expense of none. This is not a choice. This is not weighing options. This is seeing so clearly that only the best option remains, which means it is no longer an option at all. This is the freedom of being that comes when the addiction of having no longer enthralls you. This isn't freedom of choice—for all choice is conditioned by "me"—this is the freedom of choicelessness.

YES, AND

I studied improv for a year at Tel Aviv University. I wasn't good at it, and the reason was that I sought to control every situation. I couldn't accept what was presented to me and would willfully shift the scene toward something with which I felt more comfortable. I couldn't accept the *li* (intrinsic order) of a scene and sought to force my own sense of *tsu* (imposed order) on it and the other people playing it. My attitude was "no, but" rather than "yes, and."

In *Getting to "Yes And": The Art of Business Improvisation*, authors Bob Kulhan and Chuck Crisafulli show us how "yes, and" plays out:

> In the realm of comedic improvisation . . . "Yes" repre-sents the unconditional acceptance of an idea that has been presented and established by another performer or a group of performers. "And" means that you take that expressed idea and build directly on it. What this means onstage is that if one performer says, "Wow, it's hot in this kitchen," the second performer does not say, "No, it isn't—I'm freezing," or 'We're not in the kitchen. We're in a cruise ship bathroom." Both of these statements deny, negate, and otherwise undermine the offer the first

performer brought to the table. A "Yes, and . . ." response instead might be, "Yes, it is hot. And the fact that I set the house on fire probably isn't helping any."[1]

The yes in "yes, and" is being surrendered to reality. What is true of improvisational theater is true of every moment of your life: you are presented with a situation and your only option (which, of course means it's choiceless and not an option at all) is to play along. If you reject the reality of what is and seek to impose upon it a fantasy of your own making, you disrupt the flow of what's happening and find yourself the victim of events rather than their master, as you had hoped. Of course, you are neither victim or master but simply part of the happening itself.

"I say 'yes' to my addiction every time I attend a meeting and admit to being an addict. When I say I'm an alcoholic, I'm saying 'yes' to reality. I am an alcoholic. I say 'and' to my addiction when I say, 'I'm a recovering alcoholic.' The 'yes' is my addiction; the 'and' is my recovery. I can't tell you how long it took me to get to 'yes, and.' It was the biggest challenge of my life."

Saying "yes" is Step One: admitting that you are an addict and powerless to do anything about it. Saying "and" is attending meetings. If you can't say "yes," there is no need for "and." But your "yes" must be unreserved: "yes, and," not "yes, but." You must say "yes" without hesitation, without premeditation, without first coming up with a way out.

"I live my life looking for an escape hatch. No matter what's happening, I'm always devising a way out if things don't go the way I want them to go. Sometimes in a meeting or at a party I go to the trouble of setting a reminder on my phone so that I get interrupted by the beep. That way I can look at my phone and either excuse myself and exit the situation on the pretense that I have to deal with some urgent matter, or, if I like what is happening, I can shake my head and say I'll deal with it later and continue engaging with what is happening. But whether I use my phone or not, I've always got a way out. My life is one escape after another. Of course, my biggest escape is drinking."

Saying "yes" is living without an escape hatch. Why do you need an escape hatch in the first place? Because things don't always—or usually, or ever—go the way you want them to go. You have a plan. The purpose of your plan is to achieve some goal you find desirable—in other words, to be happy. If you've planned well and things go according to plan, you can expect to achieve your goal and experience happiness. The problem isn't your plan but rather that other people have their own plans that may work against your plan, and that the universe itself hasn't got a clue of your plan and wouldn't care one iota if it did.

This is what we mean when we say, "Humans plan, God laughs." But this proverb misses the mark. Rather than "Humans plan, God laughs," I prefer, "Humans plan, God weeps." When you say, "God laughs," the God you imagine laughing is mocking you: "You think I care about your plans? You think I will move heaven and earth to help you achieve whatever it is you desire?" When you say, "God weeps," the God you imagine has compassion upon you: "Don't you see that you are working against reality? Do you still cling to your own power and imagine you are in charge? Please wake up and stop the suffering your planning creates for yourself and so many others."

Twenty-six hundred years ago Siddhartha Gautama, the historical Buddha, taught the facts of *dukkha*, *samudaya*, *nirodha*, and *magga*: suffering, the rising of suffering, the ending of suffering, and the way to end suffering. In the Buddhist context, life is intrinsically painful or unsatisfying because you insist reality be other than it is. If you wish to end this suffering, you must live with what is, and the way to live with what is, is to live the Eightfold Path of Buddhist philosophy and practice. Recast in the context of recovery you might put it this way: You suffer because you are addicted to playing God. If you want to end this suffering, you must cease playing God. If you wish to cease playing God, live the Twelve Steps, especially Steps One, Two, and Three, since these reveal the madness of playing God. Most people refuse to quit playing God even while they work the Twelve Steps.

When you play God you say "No" or, at best, "Yes, but" to reality. When you cease playing God you say, "Yes, and" to reality. But you will only say "Yes, and" when your "Yes, but" drops you on your butt so often that you can no longer pretend this is a working strategy for a life well lived.

When you say "Yes" to reality you do so without any sense of security. When you say "Yes" to love, you leave yourself open to heartbreak. When you say "Yes" to an investment, you leave yourself open to financial loss and even bankruptcy. When you say "Yes" to friendship, you leave yourself open to betrayal. When you say "Yes" with your eyes, mind, and heart wide open to the possibility of success and failure, you don't need an escape hatch because there is nothing from which you need to escape.

Burt said to me, "If you work the steps thinking you will never again eat compulsively, when you compulsively overeat—and you will!—you will blame the steps and abandon them. If you work the steps knowing you may once again compulsively overeat, when you compulsively overeat—and you may—you won't blame the steps or abandon them. And you won't blame yourself either. You'll simply note that you are compulsively overeating again, and then get back to Step One."

Saying "Yes" is opening yourself to the ten thousand joys and the ten thousand sorrows without any notion that the latter can be avoided. Saying "and" is working with the ten thousand joys and the ten thousand sorrows in such a way as to not make either ten thousand and one. Saying "Yes, and" is engaging reality as it presents itself to you in this and every moment without hesitation. Saying "Yes, and" is only possible when you understand the nature of nature and no longer insist it be other than it is.

"I thought working the Twelve Steps would bring me what Saint Paul called 'the peace of God which surpasses all understanding' (Philippians 4:7) I was wrong. What it brought me was an understanding beyond all my lesser understandings that turned out to be the peace of God."

Nature is *tohu va vohu*: wild, chaotic, and forever forming and emptying and forming and emptying again. When I lived in California, forming and emptying often manifested as earthquakes. Earthquakes happen because the semi-molten lava flowing beneath the earth's outer crust moves the tectonic plates that are the earth's crust, causing them to bump into each other, or distance themselves from one another, or just grind up against one another. When these things happen, the earth quakes. The shifting plates are not a bug but a feature of the earth.

Metaphorically, reality is the molten lava flowing just beneath the illusion of power, control, security, and certainty you imagine is your reality. When reality's fluidity undermines your fixity, everything quakes and crumbles. This crumbling—you might call it hitting rock bottom—is necessary to your own flourishing. Unless and until you learn to live with the fluid nature of life, and the intrinsic insecurity fluidity necessitates, you will continue to say "No" to reality and cling to the illusions you prefer to reality. Saying "yes" is living with insecurity; saying "and" is flourishing in the midst of it.

ROCK BOTTOM

Rock bottom is the gift of quaking and collapsing. It is what happens when you truly understand that life is unmanageable.

"This is what I know: the real block to getting sober is my fear that without my addiction to hold me together, I'd fall apart, and I'm so afraid of falling apart that I would rather die an addict than discover the true me encased in the faux me that fears falling apart."

Rock bottom is a momentary shattering of everything you hold sacred: the God of your understanding, the reality of your understanding—everything that feeds the illusion of "me." It is momentary because almost as soon as you hit rock bottom you begin to frantically rebuild the shattered "me." Hitting rock bottom shatters "me" and the God that "me" worships. But it doesn't shatter your desire to worship that God, to maintain control by continuing to play God. As soon as the game of playing God resumes, another rock bottom awaits.

"I don't *believe* in rock bottom. I *experience* rock bottoms.
There was a time when I thought rock bottom was once
and for all. Now I suspect it is once and again and again
and again."

As long as you create a "me," you must also create a floor
to support it. The floor is both psychological and spiritual. To
believe in "me" you must also believe in the many stories you
tell about "me:" the isms and ideologies that define "me," and
the gender, racial, ethnic, tribal, political, and religious narratives that provide "me" with a sense of place and purpose. As
you pile narrative upon narrative, the floor begins to sag, and
in time it breaks, sending you crashing downward again.

"Rock bottom for me was working at a restaurant and
secretly devouring the half-eaten desserts patrons left
on their plates. It took me a long time to even recognize
what I was doing, and even when I did, I still found
myself doing it! And when at last I stopped doing that, I
discovered I was doing something else no less crazy. For
me there was no one rock bottom; for me there is only a
series of rock bottoms."

Think of it this way: you aren't falling to the bottom but
through one bottom after another. There is no end to it as long
as you imagine a "me" that can put an end to it by playing
God. Being "me" and playing God go together. Being "me"
and playing God seems to put you at war with your addiction,
but in truth it puts you at war with the idea of your addiction
and the idea that you should be without addictions. When
you stop being "me" and stop playing God, you at last face the
truth of addiction and begin recovering.

"My problem isn't that I gamble compulsively, my problem
is that I gamble poorly. If I was better at picking the
ponies, and paying attention to the cards, I'd win. And
if I won regularly enough, if I won big enough, my wife
wouldn't say I have a problem. She'd be out celebrating
that I have a skill. So my problem isn't gambling; my
problem is losing. No wait, that's not quite it. My problem
isn't losing, my problem is thinking I can win."

KILLING "ME"

Jesus said, "If you want to be my student, you must deny yourself, take up your cross, and follow me. If you think you can
save your life, you will lose it, but if you lose your life for my
sake, you will find it" (Matthew 16:24–25).

Denial of self is not to be confused with asceticism. Jesus
wasn't an ascetic. He ate and drank with men and women of
high rank and low. To deny yourself as Jesus intends is to see
through the self you imagine yourself to be—the narrow mind
of "me" with all its labels and narratives—and discover the
I'ing you always and already are: the spacious mind free from
all labels and narratives. What is the cross Jesus challenges
you to shoulder? Nothing other than the means to your own
crucifixion, to the crucifixion of narrow mind.

Following Jesus means following him first to Gethsemane,
the garden of renunciation where your will is surrendered
to God's will through the realization that there is no way to
save "me" (Luke 22:42). From Gethsemane, you proceed to
Golgotha, the hill of crucifixion, where narrow mind dies:
"It is finished" (John 19:30). From Golgotha, you are carried
(not by your own power!) to the tomb of Joseph of Arimathea

where the shattered "me" is laid to rest and a time of unknowing happens (Matthew 27:57–61). Finally, from this moment of unknowing you move to the moment of resurrection (Luke 24:3) when spacious mind arises, and you find yourself at home in and as the singular I'ing in which we all live and move and have our being (Acts 17:28).

The key is to lose your life for Jesus's sake (not the crucified Jesus of narrow mind but the resurrected Christ of spacious mind) and not your own. If your spiritual practice is for your own sake, if you work the steps to get somewhere and to preserve the "me" you imagine yourself to be, then there is no resurrection, no awakening, no healing, no realization of wholeness. But if you lose your "me" for Christ who is the Tao, the Truth, and the Life (John 14:6), you awaken as the Tao, the Truth, and the Life. The problem is you can't do any of this.

"I've been a Christian all my life. When I was an alcoholic I worshipped Christ and prayed to him after every alcohol-induced blackout to save me from this demon. When I became a recovering alcoholic I followed Christ but I didn't expect he would lead me to my own crucifixion. When he did I hated him for it, and then I died. He crucified me the way the Romans crucified him. I died to the whole game of drunk/sober and then I was resurrected but to what I can't say. I was still a recovering alcoholic but I was something new and something more as well. No words for that."

Jesus was a unique "me" the way you are a unique "me." But Christ is the infinite I'ing common to us all. When Jesus says, "Father, if you are willing, remove this cup from me" (Luke 22:42), he isn't asking God to spare him the horror of crucifixion. The cup isn't his looming death but his sense of separate self. This is what Jesus asks God to remove: every-thing that keeps him from fully realizing Christ conscious-ness (1 Corinthians 2:16), his own divinity. This is why Jesus goes on to say, "Yet not my will, but Your will be done" (Luke 22:42). Again, Jesus isn't saying, "God, if you don't want to spare me crucifixion, then okay, I'm willing to be crucified." Jesus is saying, "God, is it your will to empty the cup of self of each us that we no longer operate from 'my will' but 'Your will'? The answer is 'yes.'"

EVERYTHING SHATTERS

When I first entered Overeaters Anonymous, I was told that true rock bottom, the rock bottom that would at last cause me to surrender to a higher power, was once and for all. Of course, if I strayed and ceased working the steps, I would fall back into my addictive behaviors and experience rock bottom again, but if I was loyal to the steps my worst days were behind me. My own experience is otherwise: even when I work the steps and eat sanely, there are still moments of rock bottom, just not those dealing with food. Food, alcohol, sex, gambling, drugs are symptoms of a greater disease: the disease of control. The cleaner my eating, the clearer it became that something else was wrong. This something else is baked into the cake of narrow mind (pun intended); it is part of the very nature of "me." Because you cannot live without narrow mind, rock bottoms go on and on. The key is not to resist them but, as Jesus taught us, to understand them as the will of God.

Rock bottom isn't only associated with addiction. We are talking about all kinds of shattering. While some may indulge themselves in the game of "My Shattering Is Greater Than Your Shattering," it is better not to compare horror stories but rather to learn how to navigate whatever horror you happen to encounter.

"I think my drinking was triggered by hitting rock bottom rather than the other way around," a middle-aged woman explained in an AA meeting. "It was the death of Katie, my three-year-old daughter, that sent me to the bottle. If I had a predilection for alcoholism before her death, I was unaware of it. I was barely a social drinker. But alcohol became my priest after my priest told me that Katie's death was God's will. If her death was God's will, then God's death is my will. I drank to fill the void left by the death of my Katie and my God."

This is what the psychotherapist Susan Anderson calls "shattering," an experience of "shock, pain, and panic that leaves you suddenly bereft of life's worth and meaning. You try to keep the shards of yourself together, but in spite of all your efforts, your faith and trust have been shattered."[1]

Anderson's focus is on emotional trauma arising from the sense of abandonment resulting from the loss of a relationship. But her notion of shattering has broader implications. I'm using it here to recognize that rock bottom is a shattering of everything you imagine is true: "me," the God of your understanding, your pretenses, your hopes, and self-power. Shattering leaves you broken and dying on the cross. Shattering calls forth the final cry of the crucified "me": "My God, my God, why have you forsaken me?" (Matthew 27:46; Mark 15:34; Psalm 22:1).

The God who abandoned Jesus was the God of Jesus's understanding: "my God." In the context of Twelve-Step spirituality, this God was your last hope. Having failed to avoid crucifixion, you at least hold on to the delusion that the God of your understanding will save you from the madness you have created for yourself. But this God is being crucified right along with you. "My God" dies on the cross; "my God" is shattered when you hit rock bottom. It cannot be otherwise since "my God," the God of your understanding, is simply a projection of the "me" you imagine yourself to be. As long as you cling to "me," you cling to the God of your understanding. But as soon as "me" is shattered, so is the God you imagined to support it.

This is the dark night of the soul: that moment when you can no longer depend on the God of your understanding. You are left at the mercy of the God beyond your understanding. Since this God is beyond your understanding, it feels as if you are bereft of God altogether. But you aren't. You are at last free from the addiction to playing God and ready to awaken to the God who is playing you.

PART 2

We Came to Believe That a Power Greater Than Ourselves Could Restore Our Sanity

CAME TO BELIEVE

The key to understanding the importance of Step Two and its reference to a power greater than ourselves is to read it in the light of Step Three's notion of God as we understand God. These two ideas are not synonymous. In fact, they are mutually exclusive. A power greater than ourselves is a power beyond our understanding, while God as we understand God is nothing other than a God of our understanding.

"It took me a while before I realized that I can't imagine a power greater than myself. Everything I imagine is simply a projection of myself. God, which is my shorthand for this greater power, is never the God of my understanding because the God of my understanding is merely a projection of or an extension of my understanding. If I could understand God—the real God, the God who is greater than me and anything I can imagine—I would be God."

Step Two asks that we come to believe in this power greater than ourselves. But how does this belief come about?

As my sponsor Burt taught, there are three ways to engage in the believing of Step Two: desperation, reason, and intuition.

BELIEVING OUT OF DESPERATION

"I remember working Step Two in a flash. OK! OK! OK! I believe, I swear I believe. I don't know who it is or what it is or what religion it is or if religion even matters, I just promise to believe as long as I'm saved. This was what my sponsor called Step Two in a foxhole. There are no atheists in a foxhole, but the belief of the atheist is only as deep as the foxhole itself."

Coming to believe out of desperation is common but brief. As you attend meetings and deepen your recovery, your sense of being desperate eases and with it your belief. Belief as the result of desperation is an existential grasping at straws in hopes that something, or rather Something, will save you from yourself and the addictive "me" that is yourself. In this case, it doesn't matter what you believe in as long as you believe that whatever it is can save you. The problem with this aspect of believing is that it is shallow.

"The God of my understanding has changed many times. At first I imagined God as Christ, then as a more generic Divine Being unattached to any religion. Then I went into a theological funk where the only 'God' I could come up with is the Twelve Steps themselves. Now I know that whatever the God of my understanding is today, it isn't really God."

BELIEVING OUT OF REASON

"I'm not much of a believer. I'm a philosopher, a rationalist. When I started working Step Two I had no truck with belief. Then my sponsor told me to substitute the word *hypothesis* for *belief*. She suggested I understand Step Two as 'Came to investigate the hypothesis that there was a power greater than myself that could restore me to sanity.' This was a hypothesis to test, not a belief to hold unquestionably. What I came up with was this: If, since I cannot manage my addiction, there is no greater power on whom I can rely to do that for me, then recovery is a scam and I should abandon the steps and meetings. Since I saw that people did recover or were recovering I knew that recovery is not a scam. And if recovery requires a greater power than I will hold out the possibility that such a power exists. That's as much of belief as I could muster."

Coming to believe out of reason is stronger than coming to believe out of desperation, but its roots are still not all that deep. As Burt put it to me more than once: "There is no reason to believe in reason." That is to say, you cannot prove reason is the best way to determine what is so. In fact, science is coming to the point where it can see the limitations of reason:

> One of the most amazing aspects of modern science, mathematics, and rationality is that they have matured to the level where they are able to see their own limits. As of late, scientists and mathematicians have joined philosophers in discussing the limitations of man's ability to know the world.[1]

BELIEVING OUT OF INTUITION

By intuition I mean a knowing that is transpersonal: you didn't imagine it or rationally work it out; you simply awoke to it. The truth of this intuition is rooted in the same sense that you know the world you experience when awake is more real than the world you experience when dreaming.

> Since no empirical method can objectively test realness, we have to turn instead to the more subjective approach of the philosophers. After centuries of inquiry, philosophers have come to suggest that true reality possess an unmistakable quality . . . what's real simply feels more real than what's not. This may seem an unsatisfyingly soft standard, but it is the best guidance that the greatest minds and experts have produced.[2]

My dream life is quite vivid. When I'm in a dream state the world produced by that state is very real to me, but as soon as I wake up I know it wasn't real at all, and the world into which I awake has a quality of realness that trumps that of the dream state. For some, this waking state is the highest level of reality they know. The world revealed in this state is the world of "me," the world of labels, isms, and ideologies, the world in which playing God is what it is to be "me." But there is an even higher reality than this waking-state world. This is the reality Albert Einstein called "cosmic religious feeling."

> It is very difficult to explain this feeling to anyone who is entirely without it, especially as there is no anthropomorphic conception of God corresponding to it. The individual frees that nothingness of human desires and aims and the sublimity and marvelous order which reveal themselves both in Nature and in the world of

thought. He looks upon individual existence as a sort of prison and wants to experience the universe as a single significant whole.[3]

You don't come to this cosmic religious feeling out of fear or reasoned logic. You come to it out of intuition: a knowing simply arises effortlessly and you "just know" it is true and truer than the waking world the way you know the waking world is truer than the dream world. I realize this is what some might call mushy thinking, but I would go further: it isn't thinking at all. It is simply a flash of awakening happening by itself, of itself, and without any effort on your part whatsoever; it is a gift of grace that happens in, with, and as the surrendered mind.

I once asked Burt about this knowing. He said that he experienced it often, not once in a while or once and for all, but once, and once, and once again. "But how do you know it's real," I pushed him. "How do you know you are about to sneeze the moment before you sneeze? You just know. And then you sneeze."

CAME TO BELIEVE

Step Two seems to suggest there is a method for coming to believe in this transpersonal power or to induce this cosmic religious feeling. There are certainly many practices that claim to do this: yoga, meditation, chanting, prayer, for example. While all of these have proved helpful to me at one time or another in my life, none of them produced Einstein's cosmic religious feeling. The reason for this is simple: this feeling, this power, cannot be produced. It always and already exists. You are no more capable of willing yourself into Oneness than you are in willing yourself out of your addiction. But it does come.

"I devoted years to my daily meditation practice, but I never experienced a moment of awakening sitting on my cushions. On the contrary, whenever such a moment arose it was always off the cushion: walking in the woods, cleaning a toilet, changing a diaper. This never led me to stop my practice; it only freed me from the delusion that I was practicing to get something, to achieve something. Now I sit just to sit. I approach the Twelve Steps the same way: I work the steps just to work the steps. I leave recovery to a greater power."

Coming to believe intuitively in a power greater than ourselves happens on its own. You can't make it happen, and any effort you expend in making it happen actually makes the happening all the more difficult.

CHAPTER 9

A POWER GREATER
THAN OURSELVES

The power greater than ourselves restores us to sanity. Sanity is the realization of the truer world of Einstein's cosmic religious feeling without erasing the less true world of the "me" you imagine yourself to be. The sane mind is spacious mind, the surrendered mind: the mind shorn of illusion, in concert with reality, that no longer plays at being God but realizes God is playing as it. To be sane is to be surrendered, and to be surrendered requires you to relinquish the deception of "me."

The power that surrenders the self cannot be the self because the self cannot surrender itself. The self of narrow mind, the "me" addicted to autonomy and control, to the fantasy of the will, cannot give up that fantasy without imploding. The extent to which we cling to this fantasy is the extent to which we are lost in insanity; the moment we understand that the fantasy is a fantasy is the moment we return to sanity. Yet we cannot will ourselves to relinquish our will. The relinquishing can only happen when we admit that our will is inadequate; when we admit that we are completely and totally overwhelmed.

And we are overwhelmed. We always have been. Not just by addiction but by everything, by the sheer exuberant nature of reality itself. No matter what we do, reality will not come to heel. So it is that the power greater than ourselves cannot be named in any meaningful way, by Bill W. or by anyone else. To name something is to limit it, to box it in, to say "you are this and not that." Further, to name something is to separate yourself from it. To say, you are you is to say you are not me. But reality isn't this or that. Reality is this *and* that, you *and* me. So it is that recognizing reality frees us of the illusion of self, for selfhood exists only in the tension of "me" versus what "me" calls "not me."

This power greater than ourselves is what Bill W. calls "the new God-consciousness within":

> I was to test my thinking by the new God-consciousness within. Common sense would thus become uncommon sense. I was to sit quietly when in doubt, asking only for direction and strength to meet my problems as He would have me. Never was I to pray for myself, except as my requests bore on my usefulness to others. Then only might I expect to receive. But that would be in great measure.[1]

God-consciousness is pure awareness, the I'ing of pure subjectivity that cannot be the object of any understanding because it cannot be an object at all. What Bill W. is testing isn't God-consciousness itself but his thinking. He is putting his understanding and the God of his understanding under the microscope of God-consciousness. When he does, he finds that both "me" (Bill) and the God of Bill's understanding dissolve into nothingness.

THE END OF HAVING

At the root of all addiction is the hunger for having; at the root of all recovery is being surrendered to being. Addicted to having, you play God. Surrendered to being, you are God.

"I used to laugh at the very notion of a shopaholic. It made no sense to me that people shopped compulsively. I mean. 'to buy or not to buy' was not my question. And then a friend came over to help me organize my garage to make room for a billiard table. He started asking me about all these unopened boxes from different online retailers. I had no idea what was in them. He just stared at me as I just stared at the dozens of boxes containing God-knows-what that I had bought without even realizing it. 'You've got a problem, buddy,' he said to me. To prove him wrong I vowed to buy nothing but food and gas for one week. Almost as soon as I made this vow I felt this terrible emptiness in my gut. 'To buy or not to buy' was not my question; my motto was 'I shop therefore I am.'"

When you stop playing God you realize you are God, albeit not all of God. When you are freed from the endless quest for having and having more, and are surrendered to the simple fact of being, you perceive the truth that you are not apart from Absolute Reality but a part of Absolute Reality. This shift puts an end to having, to craving, to mindless consuming and the addictions that arise from it. What is there to have once you realize you are All?

With the end of having comes the "destruction of self-centeredness," the end of the delusion that you are in control or can be in control of your life. The *Big Book* claims "that most alcoholics, for reasons yet obscure, have lost the power of choice in drink."[2] I'm claiming something more: that you have no choice at all; choice is an illusion invented by "me" to maintain the illusion of control and the addiction to having.

When Bill W. says "our so-called willpower becomes practically nonexistent" when dealing with our addictions,[3] I say our so-called willpower is in fact nonexistent in all cases. When Bill W. says "we are without defense against that first drink,"[4] I say that we are without defense altogether, and as long as you insist otherwise, there is no hope of you ever being free. This is the secret of being surrendered: it isn't that you give up control but rather at last you cease pretending you ever had control.

SURRENDERING POWER

As the *Big Book* tells us, "Most people try to live by self-propulsion. Each person is like an actor who wants to run the whole show."[5] What we must be liberated from is the very illusion of a separate self:

> Selfishness—self–centeredness! That, we think, is the root of our troubles. Driven by a hundred forms of fear, self-deletion, self-seeking, and self-pity, we step on the toes of our fellows and they retaliate. . . . So our troubles, we think, are basically of our own making. They arise out of ourselves, and the alcoholic is an extreme example of self-will run riot. . . . Above everything, we alcoholics must be rid of this selfishness. We must, or it kills us! God makes that possible.[6]

But how? How can the God of your understanding, the God imagined by the very "me" that is at the heart of your problem, free you from that "me"? It can't, because it depends on that "me" for its very existence.

Bill W. is right: "We had to find a power by which we could live, and it had to be a *Power greater than ourselves.*

Obviously. This is the surrendering power, and it is not ours. But where and how were we to find this Power?"[7]

In the beginning you find this power in your imagination: the God of your understanding, the God who is you in disguise. Only when you discover the inadequacy of this God can you recognize the power by which you can live, the power from which all life arises: the source of all being, that which encompasses identity and yet has none.

"The God of my understanding proved to be no more reliable than any other idea I insisted was true. The God of my understanding was me playing God and denying the fact by imagining a God who was not me. But I could fool myself for only so long. Eventually I lost the God I found, and I lost him at the bottom of a pill dispenser."

Bill W. orders the steps the way he does to help us see the God of our understanding for what it is: a projection of the addicted self. The power greater than ourselves is by definition a power greater than we can imagine, a being beyond naming. It precedes and exceeds naming, but it is only through the failure of naming that we encounter it. And so Step Two, the acknowledgement of the power, is less a true acknowledgment than an intimation or intuition:

> We need to ask ourselves but one short question. "Do I now believe, or am I even willing to believe, that there is a Power greater than myself? As soon as a man can say that he does believe, or is willing to believe, we emphatically assure him that he is on his way.[8]

This emphatic assurance encourages you to move on in the process, from Step Two into Step Three, but what Bill

W. doesn't tell you is that as you move on to Step Three, Step Three in a sense collapses beneath you: you will cease to believe in the God of your understanding and encounter instead "the Great Reality deep down within us."[9] To return to what my sponsor Burt said of the steps: we're not climbing but falling. That way, sanity lies.

GLIMPSING THE UNGLIMPSEABLE

Ajazz musician I met in an AA meeting explained the
Power Greater than Ourselves this way: "The word *uni-verse* can be understood as uni-verse, one song, or better, one
note. This note arises out of silence, and it rides the silence,
and gives expression to the silence. Over time this one note
births infinite variations. In this the universe is like jazz riffing
from and returning to a central musical theme—uni-verse.
While we focus on the song, we must not forget the silence out
of which it comes. The song is the God of my understanding.
The silence is the Power greater than myself."

Encountering the existential silence of the God beyond
understanding is the gift of being surrendered. There is no
way to achieve "being surrendered"; it is a matter of grace
rather than will, effortlessness rather than effort.

"I once heard the Voice of God during a Twelve-Step
retreat. God addressed me directly yet seemed to say
nothing. At first I struggled to listen more closely, and
then it hit me: God isn't saying anything because there is

nothing to say. Words become gibberish while the silence itself speaks volumes."

YOU ARE GOD

Paul, a retired professor of world religions and a recovering alcoholic, told me, "You are the Power Greater than Ourselves. But the you I'm talking about isn't the you you imagine yourself to be. That you is playing God. When the Big Book tells us to quit playing God, it is challenging us to quit playing that 'you' that imagines itself as God. The God you already are, the Greater Power, is reality itself. This is what the Upanishads mean when they say, *Tat tvam assi*: you are that (Chandogya Upanishad 6.8.7). You can't become that because you are that, and all efforts to become that rather than simply be that reinforce the false premise that you are not that. No wonder we drink!"

While you cannot name the Greater Power, you can get a subtle awareness of it. Look carefully at this figure/ground diagram:

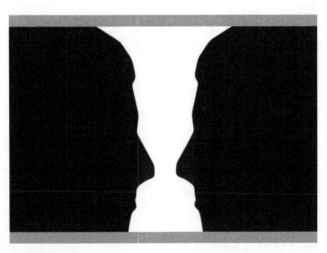

When you focus your attention on the white space you see a goblet. When you focus your attention on the black space you see the profiles of two people facing one another. Now ask yourself, "What is this diagram when no one is looking at it?"

The diagram is one thing or another depending on how you look at it. But what is it when you aren't looking? Now apply this way of inquiry to God. It is easy to say, "God is the ocean, we are the waves"; or "God is the root system, we are the trees"; or "God is the ground, we are the figure." But this is not yet the true story. God embraces and transcends all reality. God isn't figure or ground but rather figure and ground and that which embraces and transcends them both. God isn't this *or* that, but this *and* that *and* whatever it is that allows this and that to happen in the first place. There is no naming this God; there is only experiencing this God as YHVH, the happening of reality, or *Ehyeh*, the I'ing of reality: the creative process of birthing and dying, rising and falling, the ten thousand joys and ten thousand sorrows. God is both figure and ground, and the process that is figuring and grounding.

"My sponsor told me that I drink to keep from speaking. If I would just stop speaking on my own, I wouldn't feel the need to drink. While I have never managed to stop speaking on my own, I have experienced moments when I was left speechless. These were moments of intense sobriety and clarity beyond merely not drinking."

STOP SEEKING

When you speak of God as a verb and realize that all life is the manifesting of God, you realize that life too is a verb. Indeed, as noted, there are no nouns in the universe at all: just verbs, just processes, just happenings. There is nothing fixed and final, there is just *this* flowing into *that* and *that* flowing into *this*. Accepting this fact is the key to returning to sanity. Accepting comes simultaneously with seeing and understanding what you see. As Alan Watts teaches:

> You cannot get the freedom of the spirit by climbing up to it; it is not reached by any kind of ladder, for otherwise it would be possible to describe a specific technique by which wisdom and enlightenment can be "obtained" and the whole matter would be as apparently simple as buying a ticket and taking a train. . . . Now the practice of any kind of technique is going somewhere, yes, even the technique of acceptance. . . . It seems to be necessary to try to discover the secret of going somewhere in order to learn that this can never be done. The path always takes you round in a circle, back to the place where you stand.[1]

When asked to pacify the mind of a student, Bodhidharma, the fifth-century Indian monk who brought Buddhism to China, said, "Bring me your mind and I will pacify it for you." The student replied, "No matter where I look, I can't find it." "Well then," Bodhidharma said, "your mind is pacified already." The mind you seek is the mind of your understanding; the God you believe in is the God of your understanding. Neither is other than your understanding, and since your understanding is always partial, always dim, your God is always partial and your mind is always agitated. When you stop seeking after that which you project and realize instead that you are the projector, then calm is realized. Then you are sane: sane enough to see that I'ing, the Power Greater than Ourselves, cannot be turned into an object; sane enough to see that I'ing is the eternal and infinite subject, and though we use words to speak as if it could be spoken of, the truth is that Absolute Reality is always just beyond our linguistic reach.

PURPOSE

Does this Power Greater than Ourselves have a purpose? This Greater Power is reality itself: the Happening happening as all happening. In this sense, its purpose is simply to be itself. In this way its purpose, will, and nature are one in the same. As St. Paul wrote, "For in God all things happen; heavenly things and earthly things, visible things and invisible things, all powers, all hierarchies—political and natural—are created in God and for God" (Colossians 1:16). St. Paul's God is my Power Greater than Ourselves.

THE TRUTH OF PURPOSE

Burt, who happens to share my understanding of this Greater Power, once told me, "God lacks will but has direction. The direction of God is toward beings capable of higher and higher levels of wisdom, and as the Buddhists tell us, wisdom, *prajna*, always arises with *karuna*, compassion. When you are surrendered to the Greater Power, to the God who is all life, you are surrendered to compassion for all the living."

"I entered NA to get clean. I never thought about being a
kinder human being. But over time I came to see that you

can't get clean without getting kind at the same time. It isn't that the one leads to the other, but that each is the flip side of the other."

God's purpose, God's will, is God's nature, and God's nature is to manifest ever more aware, wise, and compassionate expressions of life. While God makes both the wise and the foolish possible, God's nature inclines toward wisdom. The wisdom toward which God inclines and that the wise come to embody leads to a lessening of conflict within yourself, between yourself and others, and between yourself and nature. Without conflict there is no addiction because addiction is at its very core conflictual.

"If God's nature is wisdom and the manifesting of wisdom," Burt said, "then God 'desires' or 'wills' creatures capable of being wise. If this is so, then God 'desires' you to be wise, and to be wise is to be free from addiction. Just as God's 'will' causes an apple to fall down rather than up, so God's 'will' is for you to be wise, kind, sober, and free."

If you want to understand the truth of purpose, watch Tibetan monks create a sand mandala, a symbolic depiction of the universe made with colored grains of sand. To watch them is both excruciating and exhilarating. They sit hunched over the mandala for days on end, placing each colored grain of sand in just the right spot to produce an exquisite work of religious art. Each grain of sand has its place and its purpose, but in the end, after the mandala is complete, the monks scrape the whole thing into a heap, scoop it all into a bucket, and dump what was a priceless work of art into a flowing stream of water.

The impermanence of the mandala does not erase its purpose. The purpose of the mandala was to be itself, and once this purpose was realized its reason for existence had ceased.

Similarly, with each grain of sand comprising the mandala. Its purpose was to take its place along with all the other grains of sand in the mandala. Think of yourself as a grain of sand—unique, precious, and perfectly in its place in the cosmic mandala that is the cosmos. Purpose is found when you settle into your place in the cosmos. Purpose is lost when you imagine that place is forever or that that place should be some other place.

Like each grain of sand in a mandala, you are unique and essential to life. If you pretend to be a different color or struggle to take a different place in the mandala, the mandala of life could not achieve completion. While both the sand and the mandala that arise from it are temporary, the beauty and wisdom they convey are no less precious.

Just as the purpose of each grain of sand is found in the mandala as a whole, so your purpose as a happening of the Happening is found in God. As the Christian pastor Rick Warren explains:

> The purpose of your life is far greater than your own personal fulfillment, your peace of mind, or even your happiness. It's far greater than your family, your career, or even your wildest dreams and ambitions. If you want to know why you were placed on this planet, you must begin with God. You were born by his purpose and for his purpose.[1]

The God of Rick's understanding is not the God of my understanding, but his words nevertheless ring true. Because you are not other than the whole of which you are a part, your purpose is the purpose of the whole. And the purpose of the whole is simply to be itself. The purpose of God is nothing other than being God.

How do you discover or find your purpose? You don't. You can't. That is the premise of this entire book: there is nothing you can do because it is already being done. But realizing this requires you to stop thinking in terms of "your" purpose. Purpose is God's, not yours. You are a happening of the Happening. Your purpose is to be the unique happening you already are. Warren explains it this way:

> Contrary to what many popular books, movies, and seminars tell you, you won't discover your life's meaning by looking within yourself. You have probably tried that already. You didn't create yourself, so there is no way you can tell yourself what you were created for!... You must begin with God, your Creator. You exist only because God wills that you exist. You were made by God and for God—and until you understand that, life will never make sense. It is only in God that we discover our origin, our identity, our meaning, our purpose, our significance, and our destiny. Every other path leads to a dead end.[2]

Looking within yourself won't reveal your purpose because the self that is looking and the self that is being looked at are both "me," and as such are distractions from the I'ing to which "me" is blind.

KNOW GOD, KNOWING YOURSELF

What then is your true purpose? To answer this, as Rick Warren says, you start with God, Reality, the God manifesting you the way an ocean manifests a wave. God's purpose is to happen. God isn't the creator but creativity itself. God doesn't exist, God is existence. God is the universe forever evolving beings capable of deeper and deeper levels of wisdom and compassion—albeit with more dead ends than successful ones. God's purpose, God's nature, is manifesting beings with greater and greater capacities for knowing God in, with, and as all things. You are part of that manifesting, part of that knowing. Your purpose is to know God, the Happening happening as all happening in all, with all, and as all—including yourself. When you do, addiction ends and love arises.

"One of the weird things I found in meetings was my tendency to fall in love with the people there. This wasn't sexual or any kind of psychological transference; it was that the more honest they were with me and I with them, the more I loved them. This is what the Bible means when it says, 'Love the stranger as yourself' (Leviticus 19:34). The more honest we were with one another the more I realized we were one and other, and all of us were God."

Addiction arises from the conflict between "me" and I'ing. Addiction arises from our failure at playing God and gaining control over life. When "me" is surrendered, all of this ends of its own accord. When it does, there is only love. As J. Krishnamurti explains, "Love is a state of being, and in that state, the 'me,' with its identifications, anxieties, and possessions, is absent. Love cannot be, as long as the activities of the self, of the 'me,' whether conscious or unconscious, continue to exist. That is why it is important to understand the process of the self, the center of recognition which is the 'me.'"[3]

The sanity of recovery lies in the understanding the processes of self, deconstructing the illusion of me, and in so doing being restored to our connection with reality, a connection we experience as love.

BEYOND HAPPINESS

Positive psychology and the science of happiness are very much in vogue. Having grown tired of studying what is wrong with human beings, science is turning its attention to studying what is right with us: our virtues; our capacity for justice, courage, and happiness. While the more serious scientists doing work on happiness are careful to avoid the trap of luring people on yet another doomed march toward yet another unconquerable goal, it is inevitable that the study of happiness become a road map to happiness, assuring us that happiness is our right and should be the goal uppermost in our minds.

What we mean by happiness, and what we want when we say we want to be happy and what we mean when we say we are happy, is that life is going our way, aligning with our will and our desire. In this sense, happiness is just another addiction.

"I drank in order to make myself happy. I stopped drinking in order to make myself happy. Neither tactic worked. While I was a nicer person when I was sober, I wasn't a happier one. If I had stayed in AA to be happy, I would have quit long ago. I stay in to stay sober. Happiness is no longer my problem or my goal."

Almost everyone wants to be happy. Even people who say they don't want to be happy want to be happy; they simply define being happy as not wanting to be happy. Thomas Jefferson created an entire country based on the idea that people want to be happy. That's why he declared the pursuit of happiness to be an inalienable right endowed by our Creator, or what we might call the God of Thomas Jefferson's understanding.

Jefferson was smart enough to focus on pursuing happiness rather than on being happy. Everyone can pursue happiness; few if any of us can be happy, at least not all the time. And because we can't, we drink too much, gamble too much, eat too much, buy too much, and so forth. The purpose of addictive behavior is to fill in the gaps when we aren't happy. We want to be happy all the time; we imagine happiness is a steady state rather than a momentary high followed by a no less momentary low. When this steady-state happiness proves to be false, we compensate with one addictive behavior or another.

In so far as we imagine that the sanity of recovery is a state of mind akin to happiness, we are bound to fail at recovery.

GET REAL

I don't want to be happy. I want to be real. Being real means being miserable when being miserable makes sense, being angry when being angry makes sense, being joyous when being joyous makes sense, and being addicted to food when being addicted to food makes sense—but not a moment after. Being real, as opposed to being happy, means living in sync with the moment and the ten thousand joys and ten thousand sorrows of everyday living.

"I'm an American alcoholic. As an American I'm addicted to the pursuit of happiness. As an alcoholic I'm addicted to alcohol as my way of masking the fact that I cannot pursue happiness successfully. I drink to get happy and to avoid admitting I'm unhappy. It's hard to admit I'm unhappy when the goal of life is to be happy."

For Aristotle, happiness is the greatest good:

Now happiness, more than anything else, seems complete without qualification [complete in and of itself]. For we always choose it because of itself, never because of something else. Honor, pleasure, understanding, and every virtue we certainly choose because of themselves, since we would choose each of them even if it had no further result, but we also choose them for the sake of happiness, supposing that through them we shall be happy. Happiness, by contrast, no one ever chooses for their sake [for the sake of honor, pleasure, understanding, and every other virtue], or for the sake of anything else at all.[1]

Because you need a sense of purpose, and because you have absorbed the notion that happiness is the highest value, you too may long to be happy. As His Holiness the Fourteenth Dalai Lama has said, "I believe that the purpose of our life is to seek happiness. That is clear. Whether one believes in religion or not, whether one believes in this religion or that religion, we are all seeking something better in life. So, I think, the very motion of our life is towards happiness."[2]

The English word *happiness* comes from the Icelandic word *happ*: luck or chance. If happiness is the result of luck or chance, I have no problem with it. But His Holiness says that we can achieve happiness through our own effort:

> When we speak of this inner discipline, it can of course involve many things, many methods. But generally speaking, one begins by identifying those factors which lead to happiness and those factors which lead to suffering. Having done this, one then sets about gradually eliminating those factors which lead to suffering and cultivating those which lead to happiness. That is the way.[3]

With all due respect to His Holiness, the notion that we can train our mind and root out the factors that make for unhappiness is, to my liking, far too indebted to the path of *jiriki*, self-power, and seems to discount *tariki*, other-power. My own experience suggests that the mind that needs training isn't other than the mind that is imposing the training. To impose a method of training on my mind only triggers greater rebellion on behalf of my mind. This is the madness of *jiriki*.

If I could train my mind to be happy, I could certainly train my mind to eat moderately and sensibly. But I can do neither. Because this is so, I must be surrendered to reality. This is the grace of *tariki*.

THE STATE OF CALM

While His Holiness teaches that we can train ourselves for happiness, he doesn't think it is an easy task:

> Although it is possible to achieve happiness, happiness is not a simple thing, There are many levels. In Buddhism, for instance, there is a reference to the four factors of fulfillment, or happiness: wealth, worldly satisfaction, spirituality, and enlightenment. Together they embrace the

totality of an individual's quest for happiness. Let us leave aside for a moment ultimate religious or spiritual aspirations like perfection and enlightenment and deal with joy and happiness as we understand them in an everyday or worldly sense. . . . For example, good health is considered to be one of the necessary factors for a happy life. Another factor that we regard as a source of happiness is our material facilities, or the wealth we accumulate. An additional factor is to have friendship or companions. . . . Now all of these factors are, in fact, sources of happiness. But in order for an individual to be able to fully utilize them towards the goal of enjoying a happy and fulfilled life, *your state of mind is key*. It's crucial.[4]

Why is your state of mind so important? Because the other factors of happiness—health, wealth, and friendship—are not controllable. While your behavior can influence these factors, your health can take a fatal turn regardless of your lifestyle; your wealth is influenced far more by class, societal inequalities, and the ethics (or lack thereof) of bankers and Wall Street tycoons than it is by hard work; and friendship is impeded by endless economic and familial obligations, and the facile understanding of friendship dominating this era of Facebook. The state of mind you need is the state of mind that frees you from clinging to health, wealth, and friendship.

The Dalia Lama teaches, "[I]f you possess this inner quality, calmness of mind, a degree of stability within, then even if you lack various external facilities that you would normally consider necessary for happiness, it is still possible to live a happy and joyful life."[5] If this inner quality of mind trumps the outer facilities of happiness—health, wealth, and friendship—then these outer facilities are not in fact necessary for happiness. What you need—all you need—is a calm mind.

Sadly, you cannot secure this any more than you can secure health, wealth, and friendship.

"I imagine my Higher Power to be like Buddha: forever in a state of equanimity. I imagine that my Higher Power will empower me to achieve the same state as well. I imagine that the reason I'm not in such a state is due to the fact that there is something wrong with me. I imagine I can overcome what is wrong with me and become like Buddha. I'm beginning to sense that I spend too much time imagining."

NOTHING IS PERMANENT

If your longing is to find moments of happiness, you will find them. If your longing is to find a permanent state of being happy, you will fail. There is no permanent anything. The universe is in constant flux; everything is fluid, dynamic, ever changing, and hence not really a "thing" at all but a "happening." As Alan Watts teaches, happiness happens, and so does sadness. If you long for the former at the expense of the latter, you will be unhappy most of the time:

> For man is always bound so long as he depends for his happiness on a partial experience; joy must always give way to sorrow, otherwise it can never be known as joy. But the "experience–whole" has no opposite; all the pairs of opposites exist in it, and therefore it may be described as the total acceptance of experience as we know it now, at this and at every moment.[6]

"I tried happiness once, but it never stayed. I was happy and then unhappy and then happy again and then unhappy again. It was exhausting, but only because I wanted only half the equation. What makes me happy now—and I'm not sure *happy* is the right word—is knowing that being happy all the time isn't possible. I think it was when I gave up on happiness that I also gave up on compulsive overeating."

Accepting the good along with the bad is sanity, but it is not a state of mind you can cultivate through training; it is a gift you are given by the grace of being surrendered to reality as it is.

PART 3

We Made the Decision
to Turn Our Will and
Our Lives Over to the
Care of God as We
Understood Him

CHAPTER 13

GOD AS WE UNDERSTOOD GOD

While the Big Book seems to equate a Power Greater than Ourselves with the God of our understanding, the fact is they are two very different ideas. A Power Greater than Ourselves is a Power beyond our understanding, while the God of our understanding is merely a projection of ourselves. In the early years of his recovery, Bill W. wrestled with the idea of a "power greater than ourselves." In particular, he wrestled with the tendency to name that power God:

> The word God still aroused a certain antipathy. When the thought was expressed that there might be a God personal to me this feeling was intensified. I didn't like the idea. I could go for conceptions as Creative Intelligence, Universal Mind, or Spirit of Nature, but I resisted the thought of a Czar of Heavens, however loving His sway might be. I have since talked with scores of men who felt the same way.[1]

A close reading of this passage makes clear the distinction between a Power Greater than Ourselves and the God of our understanding: the former is the non-personal Universal Mind (or the I'ing of all reality, as I refer to it), while the God of Bill W.'s understanding, the God that aroused "a certain antipathy," was a personal God. Bill seems to have found a way to overcome his antipathy when he was introduced to the notion that he could create a God that would match his preferred sense of God as Creative Intelligence or Spirit of Nature.

> My friend suggested what then seemed a novel idea. He said, *"Why don't you choose your own conception of God?"* That statement hit me hard. It melted the icy intellectual mountain in whose shadow I had lived and shivered many years. I stood in the sunlight at last. *It was only a matter of being willing to believe in a Power greater than myself. Nothing more was required of me to make my beginning.*[2]

In other words, Bill W. realized that he could hold on to his non-personal Power Greater than Ourselves without having to sacrifice it for some conventional anthropomorphic notion of deity. The fact that most people imagine God as a person (or three persons, if one is a Trinitarian) was now beside the point. Yet the notion that you can choose your own conception of God, while at first quite convenient, is also problematic in that it runs counter to the idea of surrender so central to Bill W.'s philosophy. The God of your understanding is, in fact, a reification of your understanding, and your understanding is rooted in the fantasy of control since you get to *choose* the understanding you like. Choosing your own conception of God in this way is like choosing your own conception of gravity: it is a flight from reality into a potentially deadly insanity. But then, that's the point.

"I had no use for God before I entered Program and no
use for God as I worked the steps. God meant nothing
to me because the meaning of God was so clear to me:
God was a fiction. How often was I told 'God has a plan
for your life'—sure God's plan was that I be an alcoholic.
Or 'God is punishing you with alcoholism for some sin
in your past.' Sorry, I began drinking long before I was
of the age for sinning. God was just a way of saying
nothing while sounding as if you were saying something
profound. Then I discovered that the God I didn't believe
in was the God of my imagination. Then I stopped
imagining. And then I met the God beyond my imagining
and my understanding."

At the heart of every authentic path to awakening is a
radical element of spiritual subversion designed to pull the rug
out from under the conceit of self-power. Choosing your own
conception of God is that element. Once you realize that the
God you believe in is simply the God of your understanding,
in other words the God of your own imagination, you will find
it impossible to believe in this God at all. This isn't an accident
or faulty thinking on Bill W's part. This is his spiritual genius.
He didn't want you to become trapped in your conception of
God; he wanted you to move beyond your understanding of
God to the Power greater than all understanding, so he created Step Three as a time bomb set to explode all your theological machinations. Once you know that the God of your
understanding is simply a projection of yourself, you cannot
take it to be anything else.

As Burt put it, "This is how Twelve-Step spirituality steps
beyond self-help through self-surrender and enters the realm
of radical spiritual awakening. When you place your trust in a

God of your own devising, you are setting in motion the ultimate collapse of self-power. When you realize that the God of your understanding is the God of your own imagining, the God of your self-projection, all hope in the saving power of this God crumbles, and all that remains is the Absolute Reality beyond imagining, the Greater Power, and the liberation that is awakening in, with, and as this greater reality entails."

BEYOND WORDS AND IMAGINATION

The Power mentioned in Step Two is not the God of your understanding mentioned in Step Three. Step Two's "Power" is the God beyond your understanding. Bill W. introduces the Power Greater than Ourselves before introducing the God of our understanding to hint that the real Power that can "restore us to sanity" is other than the God of your understanding, which itself is only a God that, albeit subtly, reflects your insanity. By simply saying "Power" and in no way defining this Power, Bill W. is pointing beyond words and understanding to something greater than words and understanding.

"My sponsor once asked me, 'What did you like about drinking?' I knew the answer immediately: I liked not thinking. 'And what did you know when you stopped thinking?' Nothing, I said. 'That is the difference between being drunk and being sober: when your drunk and stop thinking you know nothing, but when you're sober and stop thinking you know everything.'"

The God of your understanding is limited by your understanding and is nothing more than a projection of your understanding. The Power beyond understanding is the God beyond names and language. So why is it that Step

Three tells us "to turn our will and our lives over to the care of God as we [understand] God" rather than to the Power beyond our understanding? This is no small question, since Bill W. tells us that the "effectiveness of the whole AA program rests on this step."[3] To understand this, and hence to understand the deeper workings of Twelve-Step spirituality, take a closer look at the way Bill W. describes his working of Step Three:

> There I humbly offered myself to God, as I then understood Him, to do with me as He would. I placed myself unreservedly under His care and direction. I admitted for the first time that of myself I was nothing; that without Him I was lost. I ruthlessly faced my sins and became willing to have my new-found Friend take them away, root and branch. I have not had a drink since.[4]

Clearly Bill W.'s act of surrender was successful, and I have no quarrel with that. What interests me is the God to whom he surrendered. God here is God as Bill then understood God. How did he understand God? As the Power Greater than Ourselves, the Power beyond all understanding. Why didn't he simply tell us to surrender our lives to the unknown and unknowable? Because few of us would have known what he was talking about.

Bill W. was using the what the Buddhists call *upaya*, skillful means. He was using language that would draw us into the liberating and surrendering paradox of Twelve-Step spirituality rather than language that would scare us away from it. When you turn your life over to the God of your understanding, there is nothing to fear because the God of your understanding is a God who supports the "me" rather than surrenders "me." So you take Step Three without fear.

If your practice of the steps is devoted only to abstinence in one form or another, this level of engagement with Step Three is good enough. But if you are curious about being surrendered and the true liberation that is living the surrendered life, you will find the surface reading of Step Three very shallow.

For example, what if your understanding of God changes over time? Would you start to drink or take drugs again? Would you have to start working the steps from scratch? Would you have to surrender to this new God of your understanding the way you did to the old God of your understanding? If so, does this mean there are many Gods? The God to whom Bill W. first surrendered did in fact "do with him as he would." If his understanding of God changed, and the next God also did with Bill W. as he (or she, if Bill's understanding of God took him in the direction of the Goddess) would, wouldn't that imply there are a multiplicity of Gods, at least two of whom were effective in removing his sins "root and branch"?

Then there is the fact that the God of Bill W.'s understanding need not be the God of your understanding. Indeed, it need not be a God at all: "You can, if you wish, make AA itself your 'Higher Power.'"[5] In the context of Twelve-Step recovery it doesn't matter if the God of your understanding is the same as the God of anyone else's understanding so long as your surrender to that God is unreserved. But if it doesn't matter who or what God is, only that you surrender to your God completely, what are we saying about God?

"Before I started working the steps I thought I knew who God was, but as I listened to people in meetings I heard about different Gods and began to doubt my own. Then I lost that God of my understanding and made the meeting my God: 'My Program who art in Meetings hallowed be whatever your name happens to be.' But eventually I came to realize that any God of my understanding could never be the real God beyond all understanding. At that point I stopped worrying about who God was and found myself surrendered to what God is: truth."

HOLY PLACEBO

If God is the God of your understanding, then God is the God of your imagining—the God you create for yourself. If, for example, you imagine God is the creator of the universe, Bill W. makes it clear that even this creator God is your creation: the God of your understanding. What you are surrendering to is simply your imagination; the Friend whom Bill W. hopes will take away his sins, is an imaginary Friend. I'm not saying there is no God, only that the God of your understanding isn't God:

> The thoughts that *seem* to come from God are not answers at all. They prove to be well-intentioned unconscious rationalizations. . . . With the best of intentions, he [the alcoholic] tends to force his own will into all sorts of situations and problems with the comfortable assurance that he is acting under God's specific direction.[6]

"No, no, no, no! You have got this all wrong!" one man screamed at me as I read this passage during a lecture. "First of all, Step Three talks about turning 'our lives over to the care of God as we—we!—understood Him.' The 'we' is crucial. We're Christians, and the God of our understanding is the Holy Trinity—Father, Son, and Holy Spirit. That's how we understand God and that's the God to whom we are to turn over our lives, and that's the only God I need because that's the only God there is!"

Is that true? Is AA only for Trinitarian Christians? Of course not. "Much to our relief, we discovered we did not need to consider another's conception of God. Our own conception, however inadequate, was sufficient to make the approach and to effect a contact with Him. When, therefore, we speak to you of God, we mean your own conception of God."[7]

What does it mean that an inadequate conception of God is good enough? What does it mean that we turn our lives over to an inadequate God? It means that the God of our understanding is irrelevant to recovery. The point of Twelve-Step spirituality isn't to surrender yourself to the God of your understanding, however adequate or inadequate that God may be, but to step beyond all Gods of our understanding to the Greater Power beyond all understanding. But you can't do that, so Bill W. offers a way toward the Greater Power without frightening you with the unknowability of the Greater Power.

As Burt taught, "What the Big Book does and what each of us must do in the early stages of practicing the Twelve Steps is imagine a better self free from addiction that will take away our sins "root and branch." You can call this self *God*, if you like, but doing so doesn't change the fact that because this God is the God of your understanding, the God of your imagination, it is not in any way the Greater Power, the Absolute Reality beyond your understanding. It is simply the highest ideal you can imagine at the moment. For Bill W., that was enough. As he writes, 'I have not had a drink since.' It will be enough for you too, but only until the time is ripe for the greater awakening."

∞

"The first time I went to a meeting I stopped at a bar
beforehand and had a drink. Just one. It was to be my
last one. Then I would go to the meeting. Of course,
there was no 'last one,' only the next one, and I never
went to that meeting. I followed the first meeting I
actually attended by returning to that bar for what was
then to be my last drink. Wrong again. My third time was
a charm—literally—I found a Cross laying on the grass
outside the church where the meeting was held. I picked
it up and squeezed it tightly through the entire meeting.
I never visited a bar again. But the thing is I'm not a
Christian—not then, not now. But squeezing the Cross
worked, so I kept at it. The God of my understanding
wasn't Christ but a squeeze toy. Still, it worked."

The God of your understanding is a spiritual placebo, and
the fact that this God can free you from addiction is an example of the placebo effect. A placebo is something that has the
capacity to soothe, in this case to soothe your physical craving
or addictive thinking. It's capacity to do this isn't intrinsic to
the placebo itself but to your belief that the placebo can, in fact,
heal you. The God of your understanding can't do anything,
let alone lift you out of addiction, but your belief that it can
will set you up for the great reveal of the Greater Power. And
this revelation is the liberation of being surrendered.

FACING GOD, FACING REALITY

The God of your understanding is real, but only in the context
of your understanding. I have been to meetings held during
interfaith gatherings where the addicts in attendance were
not of one mind when it came to God. For some, God was
the Holy Trinity; for others, God was Mother Kali; and for
still others, God was Allah. For me, God was none of these,

but it didn't matter. The ontological reality of our respective Gods was irrelevant. What mattered was the quality of our surrender to our imaginary Friend. It doesn't matter if Christ, Krishna, or Kali are real; what matters is that those who understand any of them to be God believe they are real.

After one interfaith meeting, a few of us went out to dinner. As we waited for our meal, I raised this question: "We don't believe in the same God. My Jewish God never had a Son, your Christian God is not God without Him. Your Muslim God revealed the Holy Qur'an, a revelation of which our Jewish and Christian Gods are completely ignorant. And none of our Gods incarnated as Lord Krishna to reveal the teachings of the Bhagavad Gita to Arjuna in North India. Here at our conference these differences are significant, but in our open Twelve-Step meeting room they matter not at all. Why is that?"

At interfaith gatherings it is often taboo to speak of Gods this way; there is a tacit agreement that we accept the teaching of the Hindu *Rig Veda*: Truth is one; different people call it by different names (*Rig Veda* 1.164.46). This way we can talk with one another about what we have in common without having to admit to one another that we profoundly disagree theologically. At dinner we again opted for the *Rig Veda*, and my question died the moment it was born.

I respect the teaching of the *Rig Veda*, but I understand it in the larger context of the opening line of the Tao Te Ching: "The tao that can be named is not the eternal Tao" (Tao Te Ching 1:1). While the Gods of our understanding are numerous, none of them is the God beyond our understanding, the Power Greater than Ourselves and our imagining, the Tao or reality that exists just beyond words, isms, and ideologies. While surrendering to placebo Gods may free us from our addictions, only being surrendered to the eternal Tao can free us from ourselves.

"In the early years of my sobriety the God of my understanding was simply the me of my understanding projected into the heavens, but eventually the God of my understanding and the me of my understanding both ceased to be. What was left I cannot say, but I know that whatever it is, is both God and me at the same time."

THE ETERNAL TAO

I want to spend a moment longer with the Tao, and with the line I quoted earlier: "The tao that can be named is not the eternal Tao." This opening verse of the Tao Te Ching speaks to the deepest reading of Steps Two and Three. The tao that can be named is the God of your understanding. The eternal Tao, the Tao beyond all naming, is the Power Greater than Ourselves.

"God has a plan for my life," a middle-aged drunk told me as I placed some cash into his cardboard collection box. "And it can't be this one."

"Why not?" I asked. "Perhaps God's plan for your life is for you to be a homeless alcoholic. After all, if God has a plan for your life and this isn't it, how is it that you have the power to thwart God's plan and live as a drunk on the street instead?" He spit at me—and kept my money.

At the heart of much talk about recovery is the notion of free will. While we may admit to being powerless over our addiction, we are not ready to admit we are powerless in general. And this is our deeper addiction: an addiction to the fantasy of will, autonomy, and control.

Step Three is designed to break us of this addiction by revealing it to be a fantasy. To see how this works, its useful to consider the text of the step: "We made the decision to turn our will and our lives over to the care of God as we understand God." It sounds good. Just give up your will and trust in God. The problem with this is twofold. First, turning your will and your life over to God is an act of will far more demanding than simply ceasing to indulge in your addiction. If you have the willpower to surrender your life, you certainly have the power to end your addiction. Since you already admitted in Step One that you are powerless over the latter, you are certainly incapable of doing the former. Second, the God to whom you are trying to surrender is the God of your understanding, a figment of your imagination, a God of your own creation. You are in effect trying to turn your life over to yourself. You've already done that, and you know very well how it turned out.

It's also interesting to note the grammar and word choice of the step. If it's true that Step Three is about turning yourself over to God, it seems strange that God gets short shrift, appearing only once in the sentence in an inactive role. Meanwhile, the active party, the one doing all the work, is you. You make this decision, you control your will and your life, you define God. You do everything . . . everything, that is, accept surrender.

Sure, we say we will surrender, but our language betrays us. Over and over again we assert our autonomy and control. Step Three contradicts Bill W.'s insistence that "first of all, we had to quit playing God." The contradiction is deliberate. Step Three is all about pulling the rug out from under your God playing. If you could decide to turn your life over to God, you could decide not to drink or do drugs or eat compulsively or any of the other insane behaviors we find ourselves doing "against our will." You can't turn your life over to God because "your life" is what must do the turning.

Even if you could will yourself not to be willful, the God to whom you are turning over your will is the God of your understanding, which isn't God at all but you imagining what God might be. You are turning yourself over to yourself, which is not doing anything at all.

This is made clear by a close reading of the Third-Step Prayer: "Many of us said to our Maker, *as we understood Him*: 'God, I offer myself to Thee—to build with me and to do with me as Thou wilt. Relieve me of the bondage of self, that I may better do Thy will. Take away my difficulties, that victory over them may bear witness to those I would help of Thy power, Thy Love, and Thy Way of life. May I do Thy will always!' We thought well before taking this step making sure we were ready; that we could at last abandon ourselves utterly to Him."[1]

Bill W. makes it clear from the beginning that this prayer is offered to God as we understood God. Since your understanding of God is merely a projection of yourself, the Third-Step Prayer is merely a prayer to yourself. Then there is the notion of offering oneself to this God to do as God pleases with you. Who is the you doing the offering, and who is the you being offered? Is there more than one you, or is this simply another way "me" stays in control?

Things change in the next verse: "Relieve me of the bondage of self." "Relieve" should be understood in the sense of "being relieved from duty," and not in the sense of being relieved of pain. In other words, you are praying to have the self removed by God, the Power Greater than Ourselves and not the God of your understanding, and replaced by God, the Power Greater than Ourselves, the eternal Tao that cannot be named. In this way the Third-Step Prayer shifts Step Three from surrender to being surrendered, from offering yourself to God as you understand God to having yourself removed by God beyond your understanding. The idea is spot on: your problem is your enslavement to self, to the me you imagine yourself to be. This is the self that needs to be relieved of duty. Relieving this self is exactly what needs to happen if the promise of Twelve-Step spirituality is to be realized, but the God of your understanding can't do this because the God of your understanding isn't God, the eternal I'ing that is all reality, but merely a projection of the very me that needs to be relieved. Only the Power Greater than Ourselves can do this.

"Believe it or not, I've never prayed the Third-Step Prayer. I mean, I've tried, but every time I did so I stumbled over the notion of turning myself over to God. No matter how I conceived this prayer it always left me in charge. There was no abandonment of self but rather a subtle or maybe not so subtle reinforcement of self. If I had the power to surrender to God, then I had the power to give up drugging. But I couldn't because I didn't."

I suspect Bill W. knew that many would find the Third-Step Prayer troubling, which is why he follows it with this: "The wording [of the prayer] was, of course, quite optional so long as we expressed the idea, voicing it without reservation. This was only a beginning though if honestly and humbly made, an effect, sometimes a very great one, we felt at once."[2] What is the idea we are to voice without reservation? The idea that we are powerless to surrender ourselves and are at the mercy of the Power Greater than Ourselves to leave us surrendered.

As Burt explained, "Step Three is self-destructive: the more the self tries to act selflessly, the more obvious it becomes that it is helpless to do so. Step Three is there to exhaust the self you imagine yourself to be and to allow the I'ing that is your truest self to arise of its own accord."

HOW FREE IS FREE WILL?

The more you try to work Step Three, the flimsier it becomes. But then that's what's supposed to happen. Step Three isn't about surrender at all but about recognizing that self and will are mutually reinforcing fantasies. Only when you realize that you lack the capacity to freely will your own surrender are you ready to receive the surrender you seek.

I am ambivalent when it comes to free will. While I readily admit to feeling as if I have free will, intellectually I find the idea of free will troubling. For your will to be free, there must be some part of you that wills in a vacuum unconditioned by nature or nurture. I don't think such a thing exists. I'm not alone in my wrestling, as author and political commentator Jonah Goldberg explains:

> [M]any philosophers, physicists, and neuroscientists have depressingly compelling arguments that there is no such thing as free will. Brain scans reveal that many of our conscious decisions were already made subconsciously before they popped into our heads. It looks an awful lot like free will is a story our brains tell us. But here's the problem: even if you believe that there is no such thing as free will it is impossible to live any kind of decent life based on that belief. Even if our personal choices are some deep fiction, we still have to convince ourselves to get out of bed in the morning. We are still obligated as a society to judge people as if they make their choices.[3]

Is there a part of you—the "me" you imagine yourself to be, the "me" of narrow mind—that is free from conditioning, that can stand outside whatever is happening and freely choose how to engage with what is happening or perhaps not engage at all? If so, what is it? Where does it reside? How does it function? If it is not the you that is conditioned by nature and nurture, in what sense is it you at all?

"I certainly have free will," Margaret, a fifty-something recovering food addict told me. "I can be polite to you or I can be impolite to you, that is my choice, that is my free will." Okay, I said, please be impolite to me; be mean to me, berate me, disrespect me. "You mean right now? Just like that?" she asked. "Yes," I said. "I can't," she admitted. "Why not?" I said. If you are free to be polite or not, just choose to be mean if only for a moment. Margaret gave it her best shot, but she started laughing as soon as she tried. "I just can't," she said.

The reason Margaret couldn't be mean is that the conditions for being mean were lacking. If I had started to verbally abuse her, to shame her in public, then perhaps she would have gotten angry and attacked me in return. But I didn't, so she couldn't. What seems like choice is actually the result of whatever conditions are ripening at the moment. You can be polite or mean but only when the conditions for one or the others are present and dominant.

WHAT CHOICE?

Have you ever lost your temper on the telephone and then, in mid tirade, turned to a coworker who just walked into your office or cubicle and, cupping the speaker with your palm, politely ask how you can be of help? Where did your anger go when talking to your coworker? Where did your politeness go when turning back to the person on the phone? You didn't decide to get angry. You didn't decide to be polite. You simply responded effortlessly to the situation in which you found yourself. In fact, the situation and the self in that situation are one in the same. It isn't that you are at the mercy of any given situation but rather you—the "me" of your understanding—only exists in situations.

You are not separate from the situation in which you find yourself. You're a part of it. Imagining yourself separate from what is happening allows you the conceit of being able to control what is happening, or at least your response to what is happening.

"I hear this New Age drivel all the time: While I can't choose the situations in which I exist, I can choose how to respond to them. Nonsense! You put me in a private room with access to porn, and I'm going to watch porn. It's that simple. There's no choice. If there was a choice—a real choice, not some hypothetical idea of choice—if I could choose not to watch, I wouldn't have a pornography addiction. The same is true of alcohol or gambling or any other addiction. If we addicts had real choices, we wouldn't be addicts!"

Hindus tell a parable about a man who awakes in the middle of night to find a cobra coiled on his bed. Petrified, he spends the rest of the night frozen in fear, hoping not to startle the snake and invite an attack. As dawn breaks and sunlight pierces the darkness of his room, he sees that it isn't a cobra coiled on his bed but rather a belt he had left on the bed when he undressed the night before. Instantly his terror is gone. It doesn't fade over time; it vanishes all at once to be replaced by a mixture of relief and laughter. Did the man choose to be frightened or did fear simply happen? Did he choose to be relieved or did relief simply happen? Was he something other than his fear when he was afraid, that he could have responded to the cobra differently? No, he was a frightened man when the conditions for fear were present, and a relieved man when the conditions for fear were absent. You are like this man: first one thing, then another, depending on the situation you perceive to be true.

The notion that you are some neutral character with the capacity to freely choose your reactions to situations is a fiction. The only time you imagine you can choose your response is when the situation calls forth no strong reaction in the first place. And when the situation does call forth a response, is it a freely chosen response or a reaction that happens beyond your conscious control?

"I'm an angry person. I'm also a calm person. I don't choose to be angry or calm, I just discover I'm angry or calm. If I could choose between these, I'd choose calm over anger every time, but I can't choose. How can I choose not to be angry when I only know I'm angry after I'm already angry?"

A retreat participant once asked me, "What about the teaching that there is a brief pause between action and reaction, between the situation and our response to the situation? Don't we choose how to respond in that pause?"

I never experience such a pause. You might imagine such a pause after an event is over, but were you aware of that moment of neutrality when you were free to choose one course of action over another? Imagine someone is pummeling you emotionally. Imagine further that you are aware of and present in a moment of neutrality. In this moment you can consciously decide to be vicious or kind. Why would you choose to be vicious? And if you would never choose to be vicious, was being vicious really a choice? If you did choose between being vicious or kind, was your choice really free or was it shaped by past experience? Alan Watts explains:

To be free man must see himself and life as a whole, not as active power and passive instrument but as two aspects of a single activity Between those two aspects there may be harmony or conflict, but conflict itself may also proceed from that single activity. Thus man's experience becomes whole when he sees the activity of life as a whole in himself as he is now, when he realizes that there is no difference between his own thoughts and actions as they are at this moment and the nature of the universe. It is not that life is making him think and move as you pull the strings of a marionette; it is rather than man's thought and deeds are at once his own creations and the creations of impersonal nature. Man's volition and nature's activity are two names for one and the same thing, for the doings of life are the doings of man, and the doings of man are the doings of life.[4]

There is no you outside the happening that includes you. There is only the happening, and the happening is not under your control. As Watts teaches, accepting this is the doorway to freedom:

Here there is no question of which is the mover and which the moved, for man lives his life by the same power with which life lives man. This is why total acceptance, which seems to be a response to bondage, is actually a key to freedom, for when you accept what you are now you become free to be what you are now, and this why the fool becomes a sage when he lets himself be free to be a fool.[5]

This is key to the notion of being surrendered. You lack the free will to choose to surrender. When you claim to turn your will and life over to God as you understand God, you are merely feigning surrender since the God of your understanding is nothing other than the "me" who is supposedly doing the surrendering. When you realize this, you aren't doomed but surrendered. When you realize there is nothing you can do, you realize there is nothing you must do, and that everything is happening by grace. Will doesn't come into it at all.

CHAPTER 15

YOUR WILL,
YOUR LIFE

As noted in the previous chapter, self and will are inter-
locking fantasies, illusions that chain us to our addictions.
We have discussed the illusion of will. Let us now consider the
illusion of self.

When we talk about self, we affirm a fundamental illusion: the separation of this from that and you from not you. In
making this distinction we assert an independence that is, in
fact, illusory.

The Vietnamese Zen Master Thich Nhat Hanh teaches
that nothing is independent:

> "If you are a poet, you will see clearly that there is a cloud
> floating in this sheet of paper. Without a cloud, there will
> be no rain; without rain, the trees cannot grow; and with-
> out trees, we cannot make paper. The cloud is essential
> for the paper to exist. If the cloud is not here, the sheet of
> paper cannot be here either. So we can say that the cloud
> and the paper inter-are. 'Interbeing' is a word that is not
> in the dictionary yet, but if we combine the prefix 'inter–'
> with the verb 'to be,' we have a new verb, inter-be,"[1]

If you look even deeper into this sheet of paper, you can see the logger who harvests the trees, and the millworkers who turn trees into paper. And there are the parents of the loggers and millworkers without whom we would have no loggers and millworkers. There is no end to interbeing either in space or time. Everything, always, inter-is. Simply put, nothing can exist unless everything else exists. The Buddha put it this way:

> When this is, that is.
> When this arises, that arises.
> When this ceases, that ceases.
>
> (*Anguttara Nikaya* 10:92)

If everything happens with everything else, there can be no separate things whatsoever. Understanding this, you come to recognize that what you have called your life is not yours at all: it is the universe manifesting as you the way an ocean manifests a wave.

"What kept me from entering AA was pride. I was so full of myself that I couldn't imagine a God greater than myself. I was the God of myself. As God, I had power over life and death, and it was one night as I sat staring at a bottle of Jim Beam and the Smith & Wesson 9 mm lying next to it that I realized I was wrong. I thought I wanted to kill myself, but I lacked the will. Then I said, 'If I lack the will to kill myself, maybe I lack the will to heal myself as well.' That was the beginning of my questioning the idea of self; and the more I questioned, the less pride I had; and without this overwhelming pride going to meetings became possible."

If you are to survive the next six minutes you need your lungs and respiratory system to inhale oxygen and exhale carbon dioxide. After six minutes of not breathing, your brain begins to die, and whoever you imagine yourself to be dies with it. But your lungs can't produce oxygen. About 70 percent of the world's oxygen comes from marine plants and plantlike organisms, another 28 percent comes from the rainforests, and the remaining 2 percent from other sources: your very existence depends on the proper functions of billions of other life forms. If this is true, and it is, a more accurate understanding of your physical self would have to include marine plants, plantlike organisms, and the rain forests. If you can't survive without your lungs, and you consider your lungs as part of your body, it is only logical to consider these other living beings as part of your body, for without them your lungs are useless.

Marine life and trees are no more self-sustaining than you are. They need oceans, earth, sun, rain, and the rest of nature to survive. If they need all this, and you need them, then all life on this planet is no less your body than the body you see when standing in front of a mirror.

If the earth is to thrive, it needs to remain in that sweet spot some 92.96 million miles from the sun. A bit closer and the earth burns. A bit farther away and the planet freezes. What keeps the earth where it is, is the bending of space caused by the mass of other planets in our solar system, so the solar system is part of your body. And the solar system needs the rest of the galaxy, and the galaxy needs . . . you get the idea. The entire universe has to be happening just as it is at this very moment if you are going to happen as you. So all of this is you. And all of it is happening, and all of it is happening all at once: one single system of living of which you are a part. I call this system God, the Happening happening as all happening. There is no steady state here. There are no nouns. Nor are there subjects either—which is to say, no separate autonomous actors.

As Alan Watts explains: "As soon as one sees that separate things are fictitious, it becomes obvious that nonexistent things cannot 'perform' actions. The difficulty is that most languages are arranged so that actions (verbs) have to be set in motion by things (nouns), and we forget that rules of grammar are not necessarily rules, or patterns, of nature."[2] Nature is not nouning; rather Nature, God, verbs.

As long as you are trapped in the fiction of playing God, you are trapped in the fiction of nouns, and your goal is to be the Supreme Noun. Failing at this over and over, you take refuge not in reality, but in some addiction that will maintain the noun-obsessed illusion of narrow mind. This would be much less common if our languages didn't come to replace reality in our minds; if we stopped mistaking our maps for the territory they are mapping.

"I'm a drug addict. I say that every time I enter these rooms. But my greater addiction is to the ideas I find swirling around in my head. Not just the idea that I'm a drug addict or a recovering drug addict, but all kinds of self-defining ideas, labels that tell me who I am or who I'm supposed to be. I don't choose to think these ideas, they are just there. And I have no idea if they are really true. I'd love to find a program that released me from labels."

An example of a more reality-based language is that of the Nuu-chah-nulth people of Canada's Pacific Northwest coast. Formally called the Nootka, their language consists of nothing but verbs and adverbs. Rather than speak of "house," they speak of "housing"; instead of saying "apple," they say "appling." For the Nuu-chah-nulth, and for you—once you know the truth—the earth is "earthing," the universe is "universing," you are "you'ing," and God is God'ing (I'ing) as all of it.

Once you are free from nouns, you are free from the fiction that there is a someone doing something, when in fact there is only doing. But no doing is constant; every doing is a process, a dance of oppositions. Think of reality as a symphony. With notes alone, there is noise. With rests alone, there is silence. Only the interbeing of notes and rests gives rise to music. Rests give way to notes, and notes give way to rests, and the two need each other the way up needs down and right needs left. Resting and noting forever inter-are.

EMPTYING AND FORMING

The Buddhists speak of the interplay of notes and rests as the interdependence of forming and emptying. The first-century Buddhist text the *Heart of the Perfection of Transcendent Wisdom* (*Prajnaparamita Hrdaya*), more commonly called the Heart Sutra, puts it this way: "Forming is emptying and emptying is forming; emptying is not other than forming; forming is not other than emptying; whatever is forming is emptying; whatever is emptying is forming" (*Prajnaparamita Hrdaya* 8:250b). Let's look into this carefully:

Forming is emptying tells you that nothing you see is permanent. Everything is in flux. If everything is in flux, there is no point to clinging to anything. This is true as far as it goes, but it doesn't go far enough, which is why the Heart Sutra links *forming is emptying* with *emptying is forming*.

Emptying is forming means that emptying itself is in flux. Emptying isn't a thing but part of the process of emptying-forming-emptying-forming that is the flow of reality. Being surrendered means being surrendered to this flow, and being surrendered to this flow means you are surrendered to the entirety of reality: the "birthing and dying, and blessing and curse" (Deuteronomy 30:19) and the ten thousand joys and ten thousand sorrows. When you seek to willfully surrender to

God as you understand God, your intent is to avoid curse and sorrow and surrender to blessing and joy, but this is impossible since blessing and curse inter-are, and joy and sorrow inter-are. When you are surrendered, you are surrendered to it all.

"My expectation was that the Twelve Steps would lift my addictions from me, that I would be free from craving after things that were unhealthy for me, but this isn't what I found at all. It wasn't that I no longer desired alcohol but that I no longer desired not to desire alcohol. It wasn't that I no longer desired to be depressed, but that I no longer desired to not be depressed. Without the war between desiring one thing rather than another I found myself free to engage with rather than trapped in everything that arose."

Emptying is not other than forming; forming is not other than emptying reveals the interdependence of forming and emptying. By way of illustration look at the following shape:

Is this shape convex or concave? Is it both? Is it neither? The answer depends on which aspect of the shape you choose to focus on. If you focus on the bulge curving outward to the left, it is convex. If you focus on the bend curving inward to the right, it is concave. But what is it really? What is it in and of itself? What is it when you aren't looking at it?

The problem here is one of perspective and language. The shape is clearly itself, but if you label it "this" rather than "that," you create a false dichotomy. If you call the shape convex, you're not wrong, but you're not completely right either. If you call it concave, the same is true. If you call it both convex and concave, you are speaking nonsense, since these terms are defined as opposites. So what is the shape? You can't say. The same is true of reality: forming and emptying, birthing and dying, are incomplete perspectives. Like *convex* and *concave*, they are words—narrow articulations of the boundless activity that is reality.

Whatever is forming is emptying; whatever is emptying is forming. Forming is forever emptying, and emptying is forever forming. There is no end to this dance of on and off, being and nonbeing. The key is not to separate one from the other but to welcome them both. And the way to do that is by being surrendered to the flow of emptying and forming.

This notion may seem strange to you, or only available to someone at home in Eastern ways of thinking. But the truth of the Heart Sutra is found in other religions as well. Here is one powerful example from St. Paul's Letter to the Philippians:

> Let the same mind be in you that was in Christ Jesus, who, though he was in the form of God, did not regard equality with God as something to be exploited, but emptied himself, taking the form of a slave, being born in human likeness. And being found in human form, he humbled himself and became obedient to the point of death—even death on a cross. (Philippians 2:5–8, NRSV)

"I'm a Christian. This used to mean I constantly measured myself against the ideal of Christ. My self judgment was so severe that only drugs could numb the loathing that engulfed me. Today I'm still a Christian, but I live my faith differently. Today Christ is no longer an ideal against which I measure myself but a state of mind within which I find myself."

Christ Jesus is the fully awakened human being who knows the unity of God and creation as the I'ing of Absolute Reality. Putting on the mind of Christ is realizing in yourself what Jesus realized in himself: God and you are one single and unbroken happening.

Not only is Jesus emptied of self, but God too is a process of continual emptying. God cannot be anything without being trapped in the notion of being something, and if God is something then God is limited and hence not God. In other words, if God is infinite, God must be everything and nothing, and to be everything and nothing God must be endlessly forming and emptying. God, not the English noun but the Hebrew verb YHVH (which translates loosely as "being"), is the endless process of forming and emptying. As God empties into form, God becomes you; as you empty out of form, you realize you are God. This is the realization that happens at the moment of being surrendered.

God becomes human the way an ocean becomes a wave: not by creating an "other" but by extending itself into form. Why is Jesus "a slave"? Because a slave has no will of her or his own. As Jesus says in the Gospel of Luke, "Not my will, but your will" (22:42), which is Luke's way of saying that Jesus ceased to play God and simply was God.

What is true of Jesus is true of you. When you are surrendered, you stop playing God, and when you stop playing God—the God of your understanding—you realize you are God—YHVH—playing you. As Jesus put it, "[Y]ou will realize that I am in my Father, and you are in me, and I am in you" (John 14:20). And as the early Church Father Athanasius

(298–373) put it, "God became human, that humans might become God."

"There was a time, years ago, when I believed in the God of my understanding. Then there came a period of great doubt when I was convinced that my understanding and hence my God were insufficient. Now I know that I don't understand God and the God of my understanding is really the God of my not understanding, which is the unknowable God who alone is God. Somehow I find greater comfort in 'not knowing' than I ever did in 'understanding.'"

You are the fullness of God just as Jesus was the fullness of God. As Paul wrote in his Letter to the Colossians, "For in Christ manifests the fullness of God, and in Christ you have realized this fullness as yourself as well" (Colossians 2:9–10). God is continually self-emptying, meaning there is no "thing" you can point to and say "that is God." The entire process—emptying, forming, blessing, cursing, joy, sorrow—is God. And it is to this you are surrendered.

CHAPTER 16

BEING NOBODY

Having your will and life turned over to God by God—not the God of your understanding but the God beyond all understanding—puts an end to playing God, and putting an end to playing God puts an end to playing you as well. Being surrendered is being nobody. Being surrendered is being nobody. Being nobody invites the realization that you inter-are with everybody. With this realization comes a profound sense of gratitude.

What are you grateful for? Start with the biggies: your kids, your marriage (maybe your divorce), life, a good job (or maybe just a job), family, friends—that kind of stuff. Then work on the Hallmark things: babies, puppies, daisies, sunsets, and babies playing with puppies among the daisies at sunset. But what about your shoes? Are you grateful for your shoes?

Before you answer this question, take a close look at your shoes. You may have more than one pair, so pick the pair you wear most often. If they are in your closet, go get them and examine them. If they are on your feet, take them off and have a look. Start with the soles. Are they worn down or have you had your shoes resoled recently? What about the backs of the shoes? Are they crushed from cramming your feet into the shoe and forcing the backs down to make room for the ball of your foot? When you take your shoes off, do you crush the backs again, this time with the ball of the opposite foot, and kick them off? And when you do take them off, do you put them on a shoe tree to help them hold their shape or do you just toss them in a closet, allowing the leather to crack and your shoes to deform over time? When was the last time you polished your shoes? Are your shoelaces in good condition or are they frayed and about to wear through?

Your shoes protect your feet, and deserve your gratitude, but *feeling* grateful isn't enough. Do you *show* gratitude to your shoes? Does *feeling* grateful translate into *being* grateful, and does *being* grateful translate into *doing* grateful?

The answer is in your shoes. Broken backed shoes, scuffed shoes, worn-down shoes, shoes that show signs of neglect and abuse answer the question about gratitude far more powerfully than any words you might utter or emotions you might feel. Gratitude is more than something you feel, it is something you do. Gratitude is a verb.

I'm focusing on shoes for the moment because I learned about gratitude from my shoes, specifically a pair of Rockport dress shoes. They look like wingtips on the outside and feel like running shoes on the inside. When the soles of these shoes wear down, I send them back to the manufacturer to be resoled. The first time I did this, the shoes were returned to me in near mint condition, accompanied by a handwritten letter signed by the person who did the repair.

Dear Rabbi Shapiro,

We at Rockport take great pride in the quality of our work and our product. It is clear to me from the condition of your shoes, however, that you do not. The backs were cracked from improper use; the leather was dry from insufficient cleaning and polishing; and the overall look of the shoe was sloppy. I have done my best to restore your shoes to their original condition. On behalf of all of us at Rockport who work hard to offer you a quality product, I wish you would take better care of our shoes.

These people were serious about their work and wanted me to treat their shoes as if they were my own. But wait a minute: they are my own! These are the shoes that protect my feet from all kinds of dangers: hot sidewalks, jagged rocks, broken glass, discarded hypodermic needles, human vomit, duck droppings, and dog poop—I walk in some pretty nasty places—so why don't I live the gratitude I say I feel toward my shoes? Because I treat them as an *It*, an object to be exploited, rather than a *Thou*, a presence to be honored.

"I used to think of myself as a bagel with a hole in the middle. I'd spend all my time trying to fill that hole. I tried drink and drugs and sex and buying whatever QVC was hawking at any given 2 a.m. infomercial, but the hole swallowed all of it and was never filled. I thought the Twelve Steps would fill that hole, but I was wrong. What I came to see was that the hole was simply part of what it is to be a bagel. It wasn't there to be filled but simply accepted."

SELF AND OTHER

According to the twentieth-century German Jewish philosopher Martin Buber, you encounter the world in one of two ways: I-It and I-Thou. In the context of Twelve-Step spirituality, you see the world as I-It when you are playing God, and you see the world as I-Thou when you know God is playing you and everything else

The I of I-It is like the human in Genesis 1 created in God's image to rule over all creation. This human is alien to nature, at odds with nature, and forever seeking to bend nature to her or his will. The I of I-It sees life as a means to its end, a means to achieving its own happiness. Something is of value to the I of I-It only to the extent it can be of service. When its usefulness ends, its value is nil.

The I of I-Thou is like the earthling (Heb. *adam*) in Genesis 2 fashioned from the earth (Heb. *adamah*) to serve the earth. This human is organic to nature, in service to nature, and forever seeking to midwife nature's creativity and evolution. The I of I-Thou sees each life as an end unto itself, as a unique and precious manifesting of God. To the I of I-Thou, something has value simply because it has life.

Buber teaches that both I-It and I-Thou are natural to you, but only the I of I-Thou sees the world as it is. Where the I of I-Thou sees itself as integral to and a part of the whole of life, the I of I-It sees itself as alien to and apart from the rest of life. Where the I of I-Thou sees clearly, the I of I-It suffers from what Albert Einstein calls the optical delusion of consciousness:

> A human being is a part of the whole, called by us, "Universe," a part limited in time and space. He experiences himself, his thoughts and feelings as something separated from the rest—a kind of optical delusion of his consciousness.
>
> This delusion is a kind of prison for us, restricting us to our personal desires and to affection for a few persons nearest to us. Our task must be to free ourselves from this prison by widening our circle of compassion to embrace all living creatures and the whole of nature in its beauty.

Nobody is able to achieve this completely, but the striving for such achievement is in itself a part of the liberation and a foundation for inner security.[1]

The world you imagine, as opposed to the world as it is in and of itself, is a world defined by the distinction between self and other. Look around you. No matter what direction you face, the world you see is always outside of you, other than you. Indeed, as you look around you a full 360 degrees, you cannot help but notice that you are at the center of the world you perceive.

What is true of you, of course, is true of all other human beings with the capacity to see the world. No matter who is doing the seeing, the seer is always at the center of what is seen, and what is seen is always other than the seer. This biological fact gives rise to the psychological perception that self is separate from other, and there is no way to escape it. Nevertheless, the separation, the distinction between self and other, is a kind of delusion. Operating out of this delusion you fall blind to *li*, the organic order of I'ing, and seek to impose *tsu*, the unnatural order of "me."

Yet the perspective of I-It blinds you to this truth. The primary word pairs I-Thou and I-It do not simply describe the world but, in a sense, create it. The world that is seen is not separate from the you who sees it. It is, in effect, the creation of your perception. The world you see is the world you *can* see. When striving to play God, and hence caught up in addiction, the only world you can see is the alien world of I-It. When surrendered to reality by reality, the only world you can see is the organic world of I-Thou.

ALL RELATED, EACH UNIQUE

It is important to note that there is no I, Thou, or It outside of relationship. As we've learned, this is the notion of Thich

Nhat Hanh's interbeing. Everything inter-is. Buber takes this as axiomatic: "If *Thou* is said, the *I* of the combination *I-Thou* is said along with it. If *It* is said, the *I* of the combination *I-It* is said along with it."[2]

The I that you imagine is you arises only in relationship to an other that seems to exist outside of you. When this I does arise, it can do so in one of two ways, I-Thou or I-It. If the relationship is one of I-Thou, you experience the other as a unique, precious expression of life equal in all ways to yourself. If the relationship is one of I-It, you experience the other as an object to be used to fulfill your own needs and desires. The I-Thou relationship hallows the other and feels gratitude toward the other. The I-It relationship exploits the other and feels no gratitude at all.

"Gratitude isn't something I learned to feel but something I discovered I already felt when I stopped feeling I was owed anything."

Knowing the interbeing of all life doesn't erase the uniqueness and preciousness of all living things. On the contrary, when you perceive the world from the surrendered stance you are gloriously aware that everything you see as well as you, the seer, are God happening. While no happening of God is ever separate from or other than God, each happening of God is absolutely precious and unique. As Buber explains:

Every person born into this world represents something new, something that never existed before, something original and unique. It is your obligation to know and contemplate that you are unique in the world and that there was never anyone like you in the world, for if there had been someone like you, there would be no need for you to be in the world at all. You are a new thing in the world, and you are called upon to fulfill your particularity in this world. . . . Your foremost task is the actualization of your unique, unprecedented, and never-recurring potentialities, and not the repetition of something that another, even the greatest, has already achieved.[3]

Looking at the world from the surrendered perspective of I-Thou, seeing everything happening as a happening of the Happening, the Power Greater than yourself, and knowing your place in this happening, fills you with gratitude.

"Growing up in my family I was taught to fight for everything I needed and wanted. Nothing would come without a battle, and since everyone was scrambling for the same things, I learned to fight fierce and even 'dirty.' Growing up in Program I learned that everything comes to me the way a ball rolls down a hill and comes to the valley. Good things come, bad things come, everything comes in its time and its season as the Bible says. My job isn't to grasp some and shun others, but to welcome it all with gratitude and grace."

CHAPTER 17

GOD'S CARE, GOD'S GRACE

When you are surrendered, when life and will are perceived in the context of interbeing and I-Thou, you find yourself living in God's care; that is, you find yourself living by God's grace. Grace is the shattering of "me," the narrow mind playing the God of your understanding, and the surrendering of "me" to the eternal Tao, the Power Greater than Ourselves. This shattering doesn't happen because you will it to happen. It happens because when it happens it is all that can happen.

WHEN IT CAN BE NOTHING ELSE

Being surrendered, you no longer play God; you no longer play the game of "me" wanting things to be other than they are. You are simply open to whatever arises, whatever is given.

"I shocked myself—and maybe a few other folks as well—when once I admitted in a meeting that I no longer wanted to have my addiction lifted from me. I was like, 'I'm an alcoholic the way I'm five feet six inches tall. It's just who I am. No point in being different.' My drinking was a desperate attempt to be other than I was, and to make things other than they were. Once there is no point in being different or having life be different, I find there is no need to drink at all."

You see grace happening when you realize that things are as they are because they cannot be other than they are given the conditions that allow them to be what they are in the first place. Anger arises when the conditions for anger are such that nothing but anger can arise. Unhappiness arises when the conditions for unhappiness are such that nothing but unhappiness can arise. The same is true of love and joy. This is how grace works: nothing happens until the moment is ripe for it to happen. At that moment nothing else can happen.

THERE BUT FOR . . .

As I wrote in my study of grace, *Amazing Chesed*, "Grace is God's *unlimited, unconditional, unconditioned, and all-inclusive love for all creation manifesting in and as all reality.*"[1] In other words, if God is the Happening of all happening, grace is what happens.

"If grace is reality as it is," someone once asked me, "what do you make of the saying 'There but for the grace of God go I?' Doesn't this suggest there are alternatives to the way things are, and that God's grace is an alternative to some other fate?" Yes, it does. That's why it is wrong.

Whenever I hear that phrase I'm certain that the speaker knows nothing about grace or God. God is not the supreme controller who manipulates you this way or that way according to some plan of which you may at best be but dimly aware. God is absolute reality: the good, the bad, the ugly, and the beautiful. God is the manifesting of light and dark, good and evil (Isaiah 45:7). God is the Happening happening at this very moment. The grace of God is nothing other than this happening.

An Episcopal nun I met in OA said, "When you say 'There but for the grace of God go I,' you are expressing a personal preference to not be in the situation you are observing and giving God credit for not placing you in that situation. You assume you are saved from that situation by the grace of God. The implication, however, is that the person who is in that situation is outside the grace of God. How absurd! The grace of God had nothing to do with this or that situation or this or that person. The grace of God is the gift of every situation to every person."

You might imagine that grace is something freely given, and it is. Only it isn't "something." Everything is freely given: "Behold I place before you this day birthing and dying, blessing and cursing—choose life that you and your descendants might live" (Deuteronomy 30:19). "This day" is every day, and what is placed before you is everything: the good and the bad. Choosing life is giving up on the illusion of choice and being open to receiving all, and that is what it means to live with grace.

This is what Job tells you when he says, "Should we not accept the good and the bad from God?" (Job 2:10). God is the Happening happening as all happening. Sometimes you like what is happening, so you call it "good." Sometimes you don't like what is happening, so you call it "bad." Living with grace is being open to it all.

"I used to think that if I worked the steps and waited patiently, my recovery would come through the grace of God. Then I realized that my addiction was also the grace of God. At that moment I abandoned my patient waiting and found myself already in recovery."

GRACE HAPPENS

Alan Watts explains one aspect of what makes accepting grace so difficult:

> The Grace of God is offered freely to all, but through pride man will not accept it. He cannot bear the thought that he is absolutely powerless to lift himself up and that the only chance of salvation is simply to accept something which is offered as freely to the saint as to the sinner. If nothing can be done to earn this Grace it seems to set all man's self-imposed ideals at naught; he has to confess himself impotent, and this is more that he can bear. So the gift of Grace is tacitly ignored, and man goes on trying to manufacture it for himself.[2]

Watts is talking here about playing God and ignoring God's grace in favor of your own will. Bill W. told you to stop playing God. When you do, you stop trying to control what you receive and instead welcome whatever is given. What is given is reality itself, the ten thousand joys and ten thousand sorrows of everyday living. This is grace. Realizing this isn't turning yourself over to God's care but rather discovering that regardless of what is happening you are always and already in God's care.

MONK BEGGING FOR FOOD

Living gracefully, living in God's care, means taking what is called in qigong, the ancient Chinese wellness practice, the stance of Monk Begging for Food: standing erect, knees slightly bent to maximize your ability to maintain your balance in an ever-shifting landscape, arms extending outward, hands open, palms up, and ready to receive the ten thousand joys and ten thousand sorrows of everyday life.

"I used to want to be happy. That meant getting the things
I wanted and avoiding the things I didn't want. Today I
no longer make happiness a goal. I simply accept what
comes without resistance. As it turns out, it is this attitude
that actually makes me happy."

Grace happens. It isn't willed, bestowed from on high, or in any way manipulated. Jesus alludes to this when he says that just as the sun shines on the good and evil, and rain falls on the just and unjust, so God's grace is for everyone (Matthew 5:45). While it is true that the sun shines on the good as well as the wicked, it is also true that darkness befalls them both as well. While it is true that rain allows life to flourish, it also floods and drowns. In other words, grace isn't the bestowing of blessing but the bestowing of reality: sometimes good, sometimes bad, and always out of your control.

"God is one wicked son of a bitch," Katherine said in a hushed voice after a meeting. "It took my mom close to twenty years to get sober, and when she did she was diagnosed with cirrhosis of the liver and died within a year. I mean, I know she drank herself to death, but she had stopped drinking, for God's sake. You'd think God would have rewarded her for that. Don't get me wrong, I love being in Program—it works for me. It's God I can't stand."

The God of Katherine's understanding is a punishing God, but was her mother's illness a punishment or merely the inevitable result of her drinking? Grace is the gift of reality. Reality is what arises when the conditions for what arises are such that what arises must arise. God didn't give Katherine's mother liver disease. Her drinking, coupled with her genetic predispositions, simply created the conditions for liver disease to happen. I'm not saying her mother gave herself liver disease; no one gave her liver disease. Liver disease was the natural result of her condition. There is no one in control. God isn't punishing anyone or rewarding anyone but rather gifting everyone with everything when the conditions for something are such that this something must happen.

GRACE AND THE GAME

The process of happening is God's grace, which is not other than God's nature, which is not other than God's will, which is not other than God.

"When I was surrendered to God, I was surrendered to life, and when I was surrendered to life, I discovered that I had been worshipping death all along. Worshipping death was my futile attempt to shape life to my will. I stopped worshipping death the moment I realized death and life are two sides of the same coin: reality."

You don't exist. You happen, or, more accurately, you are a happening. And you don't happen apart from everything else but as a part of everything else. The universe is happening as myriads of smaller and interconnected happenings, and you are one of these. If these other happenings weren't happening as they are, you wouldn't be happening as you are. If they change, you change. And they are always changing.

Because change is constant, there is no need to change; there is only change. With every change there is a new you, a new "me," a new narrow mind playing God and grasping at the illusion of stability and permanence, and falling into addiction as a way to avoid being surrendered to the vast process of happening beyond your control. This is why you are always recovering and never recovered. You need the narrow mind to function, and the narrow mind is always prone to addiction, so you are honest and say you are recovering rather recovered. But the addiction-prone and recovering "me" is not all of you. The reason "me" can't stop playing the game of playing "me" is that "me" is part of the game and doesn't exist without the game.

"Remember that song 'I've Gotta Be Me'? 'I gotta be free, I gotta be free, I gotta be me' or something like that. I used to think that being free meant being me, then I thought that being me is the opposite of being free. Now I think that being free is being me and not being me and then being me again without overthinking it at all."

Quitting the game of "me" is like a wave separating itself from the ocean that waves it. It can't be done. The wave is not a static thing *on* the ocean, it is the dynamic motion *of* the ocean itself. There is no wave, really, only the ocean waving. The same is true of you: the narrow mind that longs to escape the insanity of the game is nothing but the game, and nothing without the game. That's why you turn your will and your life over to the God of your understanding rather than the God beyond your understanding. The God of your understanding is the God of the game that needs the game to continue, and hence needs you to continue as well. The God beyond your understanding frees you from the game by showing you it is a game.

Seeing the game for what it is—a game—doesn't mean the game itself vanishes. It doesn't mean that your suffering ends. It just means that you know that you are playing a game and need not take it all so seriously. When you don't take it seriously, you are no longer trapped in the game.

"What I like most about recovery is never being recovered and always recovering instead. Being a recovering something reminds me that I am nothing in particular: not this or that but this and that whenever this or that happens. Recovering from this and that allows me to relax when I see this and that happening. I don't cling to this or push that away, I'm just a recovering this and that moment to moment."

The game ends when the "me" of your understanding is no longer playing the God of your understanding. The game ends when you turn from delusion to reality. This turning cannot happen through will but by grace alone.

LIVE LIFE AS IT IS

Living with choiceless awareness is what the Japanese call *sono-mama*: living life as it is. As Buddhist scholar Taitetsu Unno wrote:

> *Sono-mama* is reality affirmed as it is without being distorted by calculative thinking [narrow mind]. Since it is beyond the conventional subject-object duality, it is described as being non-dual. Although *sono-mama* is beyond conceptual grasp, it can be manifested in a person's life. Anna Pavlova suggests something akin to this in the case of dancing; once she is said to have proclaimed, "The secret of becoming a fine dancer is to learn the theory and the technique thoroughly— then forget all about it and just dance." Just dance *sono-mama*, but only after mastering the theory and technique.[3]

Theory and technique are the Twelve Steps. Just dancing is recovery.

> Everything is as-it-is (*sono-mama*) means this: We undergo all kinds of difficult and painful practices. We travel to all kinds of places and then discover that we didn't have to do a thing. That things are as–they–are. It's not that everything is as–it–is, without us having tried anything. Everything is as–it–is after we've broken our bones, trying everything.[4]

The purpose of Step Three is to exhaust us, to push us through the difficult and painful practice of trying to turn ourselves over to God so that, in the end, exhausted and broken by our efforts, we at last give in to the reality of having already and always been overturned.

LETTING GO
OF DECIDING

We could read the first three of the Twelve Steps as exercises in decision-making: we decided to admit we were powerless over our addiction; we decided to believe that a Power Greater than Ourselves could restore us to sanity; we decided to turn our will and our lives over to the care of God as we understood God. Reading these steps this way, and knowing that we really lack the power to decide these things, reveals the double bind that Twelve-Step spirituality puts us in.

A double bind situation is one in which you are faced with two mutually exclusive demands. In the context of Twelve-Step spirituality these demands are (1) accept that you are powerless and (2) know you are powerful enough to surrender. You can't have it both ways. Bill W. placed us in this position on purpose. He wants us to see the madness of our situation not in order to have us change it but rather to have us surrendered by it.

As Burt put it to me, "You're damned if you do and damned if you don't."

"So what can I do?" I asked. He looked at me like I was insane, and then he started to dance a crazy hora, waving his hands over his head and singing *"hava nagila, hava nagila."* *Hava nagila* means "let us rejoice." "When you can't do anything," Burt said, "rejoicing just happens. What keeps you from rejoicing is your addiction to deciding. Just be damned, dammit!"

The comedian Katie Goodman explains it this way:

"There are reasons we're attached to the way things are. We want the comfort of knowing, of no surprises. But there are situations where we might be stuck—in ill health, for example—and not take the steps to help ourselves move on. Why on earth would we do that? Well, it's more common than you think. We get something out of staying where we are. Being sick or in pain gains us sympathy perhaps. It's hard to let go of that attachment, no matter how much we say we don't like the problem. This is true of bad relationships, bad bosses, terrible jobs, financial woes, etc. Staying stuck is a form of attachment."[1]

Attachment isn't irrational. You rarely if ever act irrationally. Yes, you might do things that turn out to be unwise, even stupid, but at the time you do them they don't appear to be this way at all. What appears reasonable at any given moment is determined by what appears true to you at that moment. You are attached to me and all the mad behaviors in which me engages, not because being me or doing what me does is irrational but because being me or doing what me does seems completely rational.

"I eat crazily, but I never feel crazy when I do so. No matter how insane my eating may look to someone else, it seems at the time to be the only rational thing to do from my perspective. Do you know where I go after attending an OA meeting? I go to Walgreens and buy candy, and I eat the candy as I drive home from my meeting. Is this crazy? It sounds crazy to me as I admit it to you now, but when I do it, it isn't crazy. It's my reward for going to my meeting."

Imagine you are swept off your feet by a flash flood. As the water rushes you along to what you expect will be death by drowning, you notice and grasp hold of a stout branch and manage to resist the push-pull of the water. You cling to the branch for dear life. While you're focused on clinging you fail to notice the people waiting to rescue you from the flood if you would just let go of the branch. But you don't. Why? Because you know or think you know that if you let go of the branch, your life will come to an end. You play God and cling to the fiction of control for the same reason: without the illusion of control you cannot imagine living at all, and yet real living comes from not being in control.

Most of us will cling to our addiction even when freedom is offered to us. Being free means being free from the illusion of control, and this is more frightening than almost anything else you can imagine. Your addiction to control is central to your sense of "me"; without the former, the later cannot stand. You'd rather die as "me" than live as you.

DYING TO LIVE

Father Thomas would cup his hands together and raise them up as if he were raising water to his lips from a fountain. "This is me," he would say, referring to the imaginary something in his cupped hands. "Whenever Thomas arises," he continues lifting his hands, "I let him go," and he uncouples his hands and drops his arms to his sides. "This is a good practice, but not yet true liberation. The one thing I cannot let go of is the me that is doing the letting go."

Letting go is an act of surrender. Letting go of the one who is letting go is an act of being surrendered. You cannot do this. "Me" cannot do this. I'ing does it constantly.

"Where do you imagine you will go when you die?" I asked Thomas during a visit to his monastery in Snowmass, Colorado. "Nowhere," he said. "All my life I have been dropping Thomas. When I die, God will drop the last of me. And without me, there is nowhere for me to go."

In Judaism, this final dropping is called the kiss of God. Speaking metaphorically, when you are born, God, the I'ing of all reality, breathes consciousness into you through your nostrils (Genesis 2: 7). This is "me" arising on the surface of I'ing the way a wave arises on the surface of the ocean. When you die, God kisses you on the mouth and in a moment of ecstatic surrendering you sigh "me" back into God. This is the sigh of Jesus on the Cross: "It is finished" (John 19:30), the "it" being "me." As I explained in chapter 1, this is a moment Hindus call *satchitananda*: pure being, pure consciousness, pure bliss.

"I know that moment," a Sufi I met in Istanbul said to me. "We Sufis call it 'dying before you die.' It is a moment of complete returning to Allah. During my lifetime each return is complete but not permanent. The turning continues: me into Allah, Allah into me, over and over and over again. At some point, however, I no longer return, though Allah continues turning. I am gone and only Allah remains."

Your greatest attachment is to the me that fights returning to Allah, God, Absolute Reality. Any addictive behavior is a symptom of that greater attachment. You drink, drug, eat, gamble, steal, to avoid the final returning, to keep the game in play. This is a mistake.

∞

"I've come to think of recovery as a kind of death, of recovering as a kind of dying. I'm dying to the addicted me and into the me beyond all addiction."

One Hanukkah, Burt sent me a cheap plastic dreidel, the top Jews spin as part of a gambling game we play at Hanukkah time. Burt's dreidel came with a note: "You are a dreidel spinning for dear life in hopes that you will at last win. The real message of the dreidel is that you will at last stop spinning. While you spin, you imagine the prize you are playing for. When you stop, you realize that the true prize is no longer being dizzy from all that spinning."

LIVING SURRENDERED

The surrendered life brings about a Copernican revolution in perspective. Prior to being surrendered you tend to view yourself as the center of your world. This is natural. Whether you look forward or backward, to the right or to the left, you are always at the center of things. Everything is happening around you. Just as Copernicus proved that the earth revolves around the sun rather than the sun around the earth, so being surrendered proves that the world isn't revolving around you at all. But neither are you revolving around it. Rather you are an organic expression of the world. You are a bit of life become self-aware with the capacity to become life-aware as well.

There are two basic ways to situate yourself in the world: alien and organic. The book of Genesis provides you with both options. Toward the close of Genesis chapter 1, God decides to create *adam*, humanity, in God's image and likeness to rule over the fish, birds, animals, reptiles, and "every living thing that creeps on the earth" (Genesis 1:26). Where does *adam* originate? While light is called out of darkness, dry land out of the sea, vegetation and animals out of the dry land, and fish out of the ocean, humanity comes out of the mind of God.

Unlike the rest of creation, humans are alien to creation and fashioned by God to rule over creation. Humanity is an afterthought with nothing to do. Creation is already thriving without human intervention, so the only thing for humanity to do is seek to dominate it. As Alan Watts points out, humankind "aspires to govern nature, but the more one studies ecology, the more absurd it seems to speak of any one feature of an organism, or of an organism/environment field, as governing or ruling others."[1]

The second chapter of Genesis gives us an alternative to the alien origin of humanity found in the first chapter:

> When God made earth and sky there were no trees on the earth, and no shrubs had sprouted, for God had yet watered the earth, and there was no human to work the soil. God caused dew to ascend from the earth and water the soil. And God formed the human (adam) from the fresh mud of the ground (adamah), and blew consciousness into the human's nostrils, and the human became a living being. (Genesis 2:5–7)

In this story of creation, humanity is organic to nature: an earthling (adam, human) composed of earth (adamah, humus), created not to rule nature but to serve her. Rooting our identity in Genesis 2 rather than Genesis 1 is the Copernican revolution being surrendered brings about.

WHY ARE YOU HERE?

Your task isn't to play God and rule the earth but to realize you are God manifesting as you to care for the earth and see to earth's flourishing. Your job is to realize the wholeness of self and creation, part and whole, and to facilitate, not manipulate, the happenings of God.

Again, Alan Watts:

Wholeness is his keyword; his acceptance is total, and he excludes no part of his experience, however unsavory it may be. And in this he discovers that wholeness is holiness, and that holiness is another name for acceptability. He is a holy man because he has accepted the whole of himself and thus made holy what he was, is, and shall be in every moment of his life. He knows that in each of those moments he is united with God, and that whether he is saint or sinner the intensity of that union never changes. For God is the wholeness of life, which includes every possible aspect of man and is known in accepting the whole of our experience each moment.[2]

The philosopher Aaron James links this wholeness to grace:

There'd be no occasion to flow freely, in heightened adaptive attunement to what is beyond one's control. . . . Am I less free for being dynamically bounded as each new moment presents itself? . . . As an embodied, embedded human being, I'm freest not when I'm imposing my will on events . . . but when I'm responding attunedly to each moment. . . . Freedom is not simply the basic condition of my conscious being but an achievement in action; not "bare consciousness" but a reciprocal relationship, the successful "exchange" between my initiatives and the circumstances that carry me along. I'm free . . . because I'm successfully flowing, adapting as appropriate, being attuned to each . . . moment, in a state of grace.[3]

"I drank because I thought drinking would set me free. Then I stopped drinking because I thought not drinking would set me free. Then I stopped thinking and realized drinking or not drinking, I am always free."

PART 4

The Surrendered Life

SERENITY

In part 4 I want to focus on some of the gifts and insights arising from living a surrendered life that help us to both deepen our understanding and our practice of the first three steps of Twelve- Step spirituality. My list isn't exhaustive, and my thoughts continue in the "stone-skimming" style. Read them slowly and contemplate each before skipping off to the next. Let's begin with the notion of serenity.

There are moments when you realize there is nothing you can do. These are the moments of being surrendered. These are moments of profound powerlessness that somehow—and I doubt anyone knows how—empower.

There are moments when I have stood face-to-face with my addiction—pulled toward food like a moth to a flame yet flapping my wings frantically in a desperate effort not to eat. The more I flap, the closer to eating I move. I must not eat, yet I cannot help myself. Then something happens. Not something of my own doing. Something happens *tzu-jan*, "of-itself-so." In this happening, my frantic flapping stops. It doesn't lessen, slow, or gradually subside; it stops. And when it stops, the craving stops with it and I don't eat. I don't eat not because I'm not supposed to eat—after all, I'm a food addict; I don't eat not because I choose not to eat—I'm incapable of making that choice. I don't eat compulsively because eating compulsively is no longer a choice. Not eating compulsively is choiceless.

Choicelessness happens when your will has been turned over, surrendered to the Greater Power in which and all which happen. Choiceless moments are moments of serenity.

The Serenity Prayer written by the twentieth-century theologian Reinhold Niebuhr is often recited during Twelve-Step meetings:

> *God, grant me the Serenity to accept the things I*
> *   cannot change,*
> *Courage to change the things I can, and*
> *Wisdom to know the difference.*

If "God" here is the God of Reinhold Niebuhr's understanding, and I'm begging this God to bestow serenity upon me as a king might bestow a boon, I'm not much interested. But if "God" is the Happening happening as all happening, and serenity arises out of the very happening of happening, I'm very interested.

Don't imagine that serenity is the result of accepting the things you cannot change, having the courage to change the things you can change, and the wisdom to discern difference. Understanding the prayer this way is getting things backward. Serenity is the prerequisite to acceptance, change, and wisdom, not the result: God grant me the serenity *necessary* for acceptance, change, and wisdom. Serenity isn't earned through acceptance, change, and wisdom. It is given by grace before acceptance, change, and wisdom in order to make acceptance, change, and wisdom possible.

Serenity arises of its own accord, liberating you from likes and dislikes, addiction and recovery—from any form of resistance to reality as it is. With serenity comes clarity and you see that what is, is because it cannot be anything other than what it is. You're an addict not because you choose to be but because you cannot choose not to be. When you realize you cannot choose not to be, you are suddenly free from choosing all together. Without the conflict of choice, you find yourself surfing the waves of what is without any thought of making what is other than what it is. Surfing reality doesn't make the ocean calmer; it doesn't do away with cravings, but it allows you to maintain balance and not be engulfed by the waves of craving that flow around you. It is still a wild ride, but no longer a deadly one.

"The secret to my recovery—and I know it is one day at a time—was the realization that I didn't have to choose between drugging and not drugging. No, wait; I couldn't choose between taking drugs and not taking them. Whenever I imagined it was a choice, I chose drugs. But when I realized it wasn't a choice, when I discovered my addiction wasn't something I choose or reject, the very notion of choosing and rejection left me. I mean, I'm still an addict, but no longer choosing to be other than I am allows me the freedom to be a recovering addict."

Shantideva, an eighth-century Indian Buddhist, addressed this issue in *The Way of the Bodhisattva*: "If there's a remedy when trouble strikes, what reason is there for dejection? Just take the remedy. And if there is no remedy, what use is there for being glum?"[1] The remedy offered by Twelve-Step spirituality is the realization there is no remedy. This is not surrendering to one's situation but being surrendered by it. Once you are surrendered by it, you are surrendered from it.

You cannot try to act without effort, for the very act of trying is effort. In judo the most important lesson is learning how to fall. "Falling is not difficult," my sensei used to say. "Any fool can do it. Falling gracefully, however, takes wisdom. Both kinds of falling are due to gravity. Foolish falling is tripping over gravity. Wise falling is being surrendered to gravity." With surrendering comes serenity, and with serenity, the invitation to grace.

FREEDOM OF IMPERFECTION

Accepting the invitation to grace means accepting the gift of freedom—the freedom, that is, of imperfection.

When I was an undergraduate studying Buddhism in the 1970s, my teacher Taitetsu Unno and his wife, Alice, would invite students to their home where Alice, a master of Japanese tea ceremony, would guide us through the practice. As each of us received a cup of tea we were instructed to turn the cup in our hands until we found the perfect and most beautiful spot from which to sip the tea. What we discovered was that the "perfect" spot was most often the most imperfect spot on the cup. "What is beautiful isn't perfection," I remember Professor Unno saying. "What is beautiful is imperfection."

The Japanese call this *wabi-sabi*, beauty through imperfection, as the poet-writer John Louis Cimasi explains:

> Characteristics of the *wabi-sabi* aesthetic include asymmetry, asperity (roughness or irregularity), simplicity, economy, austerity, modesty, intimacy, and appreciation of the ingenuous integrity of natural objects and

processes. . . . *Wabi-sabi* nurtures all that is authentic by acknowledging three simple realities: nothing lasts, nothing is finished, and nothing is perfect.[1]

The perfect is imposed order, what the Chinese call *tsu*. What is imperfect, natural, and most beautiful is innate order, what the Chinese call *li*. Embracing *wabi-sabi* is living with the *li* of reality. Living with *li* is *wei-wu-wei*, acting in harmony with reality as it is without imposing your will on it to make it what you imagine it ought to be.

The author Julie Pointer Adams breaks down *wabi-sabi* this way:

> *Wabi* means something like simplicity, humility, and living in tune with nature. . . . *Sabi*, on the other hand, refers to what happens with the passage of time: it's about transience and the beauty and authenticity of age. Practicing *sabi* is learning to accept the natural cycle of growth and death, as well as embracing the imperfections that come with this progression. Together *wabi* and *sabi* form a feeling that finds harmony and serenity in what is uncomplicated, unassuming, mysterious, and fleeting.[2]

Living *wabi-sabi* means being freed from your addiction to perfection, to imposed order, to *tsu*. Living *wabi-sabi* means being freed for living with grace, with the serenity that recognizes and accepts both *tohu va vohu*, chaos, and *li*, the natural order innate even to chaos.

"I don't know which I experienced first, serenity or freedom. I'm not even sure there is a real difference between them: serenity is freedom, freedom is serenity.

All I do know is that they arose with my sobriety though neither triggered it."

INTRINSIC ORDER

Years ago, while on retreat in upstate New York, I crossed a wooden bridge arcing over a slow-moving brook. Standing at the center of the bridge and contemplating the water flowing beneath me I became aware that the large rocks and tree limbs that had fallen into the brook were somehow not right. They weren't symmetrical. I climbed down to the brook, waded into the water, and began to rearrange the landscape. Yet the more ordered the scene became, the less right it appeared to be. Eventually I realized I was looking for imposed order in the innate order of water-rock-tree limb happening all around me. I do this all the time, and the effort I expend on imposing my notion of order on the *wabi-sabi* and delightfully chaotic beauty of nature (within and around me) is at the heart of my addiction. I walked back to the bridge and deeper into the woods, saddened by the fact that I couldn't put things back the way they were but taking some comfort knowing that in a moment the brook would find a new "right" again.

Living the surrendered life is *wabi-sabi*. You no longer live by the imposed order and instead discover and live in alignment with the intrinsic order. You no longer resist chaos and impermanence but learn to engage with it in the manner of *wei-wu-wei*, non-coercive action.

Living the surrendered life you are at peace with what is so: addiction, recovery, sin, sainthood, birthing, dying, blessing, cursing—the ten thousand joys and ten thousand sorrows of everyday living. When you are at home with what is, there is no desire to escape what is. When there is no desire to escape, there is no more need for addiction. In this alone is there freedom, the only freedom you can know.

FREEDOM FROM CONTROL

Too often people mistake freedom for being in control, when in fact freedom is being at home with being out of control. We mistakenly understand freedom as being able to impose our will on circumstances and create our own reality. Such a notion ignores the fact of interbeing. It splits you off from the world and locks you into a never-ending struggle of playing God and seeking to control the world. Living the surrendered life offers you another kind of freedom: not the freedom to control but the freedom from control allowing you to flow with rather than frantically fight against *li*, the innate current of life.

The way of *wabi-sabi* realizes that "things are either devolving toward or evolving from emptiness."[3] When you are surrendered to reality, you effortlessly accept the inevitable and appreciate the cosmic order of things forever emptying and forming. You find truth in what is, greatness in the simple and seemingly inconsequential, and you are freed from all that is unnecessary that you might live only with what is essential.

"My life became so simple after working the steps a few times. I was an addict. I was in recovery. I made mistakes. I made amends. While I still experienced trauma, I did so without all the extraneous drama that used to accompany it."

THE HIGHS AND LOWS OF JOY

I am a fan of Marie Kondo's *The Life-Changing Magic of Tidying Up: The Japanese Art of Decluttering and Organizing.*

When speaking about living with the essential, Marie focuses on the things with which you surround yourself. Rather than focus on what you should discard, she offers a beautiful way of discovering what you should keep: "Take each item in one's hand and ask: 'Does this spark joy?' If it does, keep it. If not, dispose of it."[4]

Where happiness is the goal of the unsurrendered life, joy is a central aspect to living the surrendered life. It is what arises when you stop playing God. Happiness is a prize that is never won. Joy is a gift that is always given.

"What I want out of life is to be happy. It's that simple. What I get out of life is mostly suffering. It's that obvious. I took to alcohol to mask the suffering. I thought it would make me happy. I was wrong. Sure, it numbed the suffering at first, but then it brought its own suffering, maybe even a deeper suffering. With all due respect to Thomas Jefferson and his pursuit of happiness, that's all it is: a pursuit. Happiness just never comes or at least it never comes to stay."

Nothing comes to stay. Everything rises and falls as conditions dictate. If you seek to root joy in one or the other set of circumstances, you will find joy as elusive as happiness. But if you find joy in the process of rising and falling, emptying and forming, joy is simply what is.

"There was a time when I expected to be a recovered addict—recovered once and for all. Even when I slipped off the path and found myself caught in my addiction again, I held out the notion that I could be free from this insanity. Now I experience things differently. For me there is no recovery, only recovering. And while I haven't touched a drink in years, the desire to do so still lingers. This isn't unique to me, of course, but being freed from any notion of forever drunk or forever sober has been the key to my living whole with the brokenness of my life and life in general."

BAMBOO BEAUTY

Burt and I were sitting in his backyard looking at a small grove of bamboo that had taken over a corner of his yard. "Which is the more beautiful," he asked me, "the Empire State Building or a stalk of bamboo?" The Empire State Building is among my most favorite buildings, second only to the Flatiron Building, both of which are on New York City's Fifth Avenue. The power and grandeur of the Empire State Building, an amazing feat of engineering, is breathtaking, but the stalk of bamboo is magical.

"It isn't that the former is man-made while the latter is natural," Burt said after I ranked the bamboo over the building. "After all, humans are natural and our skyscrapers are no less natural to us than an eagle's nest is to the eagle. It's that the building is perfect while the bamboo is imperfect. The Empire State Building is *tsu* [imposed order], the bamboo is *li* [innate order]; the Empire State Building is flawless, the bamboo is *wabi-sabi*."

The subtle joy of *li* isn't high, and the gentle sadness of *wabi-sabi* isn't low. There is no high or low, just high-low-high-low: the sometimes slow, sometimes swift flowing of reality moment by moment. Joy in this sense is like a mother sighing as her toddler goes off to preschool; a sigh tinged with pride at her going and sadness at her being gone.

Once you have a feel for *wabi-sabi,* you have a new appreciation for what you formerly thought of as broken. You look at an old wooden table with all its nicks, cracks, and other so-called imperfections and you no longer think about replacing it or refinishing it, but instead you find that these "flaws" are in fact the very things that give the table character. You are no longer captivated by advertisements touting the new and find a subtle joy in the old.

To see what I mean, it is useful to turn to Andrew Juniper's lovely description of *wabi-sabi*:

> Unlike many Hellenic-inspired concepts of beauty, *wabi-sabi* has nothing to do with grandeur or symmetry; on the contrary, it requires that one should observe, with the utmost attention, the details and nuances that are offered to the keen eye. For it is in these almost imperceptible details that one can find the visual treasures that lie at the heart of *wabi-sabi*, and it is through them that one might be able to catch a glimpse of the serene melancholy that they suggest.[5]

As odd as it may sound, Juniper's phrase "serene melancholy" is what I mean by the subtle joy arising from the surrendered state. When you think of surrendering to the God of your understanding you imagine this moment of surrender being accompanied by a liberating, permanent state of happiness. But being surrendered to reality isn't like that at all. Being surrendered to reality exposes you to the never-ending rising and falling of life. You see all things coming and going, birthing and dying, forming and emptying. You are softly sad—not unhappy, depressed, desolate, or miserable, but just gently sorrowful. And because this sorrow isn't at odds with anything—because it arises from a knowing of Tao and *li*, which is the way of everything and the way everything is—you are serene, untroubled, peaceful, at ease, and even joyous.

You may find it paradoxical or just irrational to link serene melancholy with subtle joy. I suppose it is, especially if you define joy as happiness. But joy isn't happiness. Joy is the soft sigh of being surrendered.

"There is a subtle joy to being surrendered in recovery. It arises I think from the release of tension I carried when I wrestled with my addiction and learned to dance with it instead. There is effort in both wrestling and dancing, but in wrestling effort is expressed as will while in dancing it is expressed as play. When wrestling you must never surrender to your opponent, while when dancing you must always be surrendered to your partner."

CHAPTER 22

INNER SEEING

The "serene melancholy" that arises with living surrendered to *wabi-sabi*, the perfection of imperfection, invites you to look at your life in such a way as to bring the gifted nature of your existence into sharp focus. In Japan this invitation leads to the practice of *Naikan* or "inner seeing," a therapeutic process of healing created in the 1940s by Ishin Yoshimoto and rooted in *Jodo Shinshu*, or Pure Land Buddhism. Gregg Krech, a leading authority on *Naikan* in North America, describes it this way:

> *Naikan* broadens our view of reality. It's as if, standing on top of a mountain, we shift from a zoom lens to a wide-angle lens. Now we can appreciate the broader panorama: our former perspective is still included, but it is now accompanied by much that had been hidden. And what was hidden makes the view extraordinary.[1]

ACKNOWLEDGING THE GIFTS
Naikan practice rests on three questions:

> *What have I been gifted from ____?*
> *What have I gifted to ____?*
> *What troubles and difficulties have I caused ___?*

Traditionally *Naikan* inquiry begins with your mother and memories of your mother from as far back in your life as you can recall, but for our purposes you can begin with anyone you choose and focus on the present. Without judging the quality of the gift or the motives behind it, with what were you gifted today by friends, family, coworkers, and even strangers?

Here is a partial list I drew up from just the past few hours. I awoke at 5:30 this morning, pushed back a blanket and sheet made by perfect strangers, rolled out of a bed made by other strangers, and padded into the bathroom to use the plumbing made and maintained by still other strangers. I then put on my gym clothes—also made by strangers—and walked to the gym about a half mile from my home. There the door was held open for me by a man I regularly see but do not know, and I was greeted by an employee (whose name I also don't know) who signed me in. I then climbed on a stationary bike I didn't make and rode seven miles while watching MSNBC's *Morning Joe* on a television attached to the bike. I have no idea how many people it took to produce and broadcast this show, or how many reporters it took to gather the day's news that I allowed to fuel my morning negativity regarding the fate of my country and the world. But all of them were gifting me with their skills and talents. My list could go on endlessly. And it does.

Having noted what I receive from all these people, I move on to the second *Naikan* question: With what have I gifted them? The answer: nothing. Okay, I pay my gym membership and that helps keep the fellow at the front desk employed, but other than that, what do I do for any of the dozens and dozens of people whose endless toil allows me to live my life? While Mika and Joe give me insight and information, I give them nothing at all.

When I focus my inquiry on people, animals, and things closer to home, I find that while I do some things for others—wash the dishes; do the laundry; clean the house; feed, brush, and go on walks with my dog—my list of gifts given to others is still miniscule compared to my list of things gifted to me by others. And that is a key point of *Naikan*: the more aware I am of how life inter-is, the more humbled I am by the gifts I receive.

Having listed all the gifts I receive from others, and the few gifts I give them, I now take stock of the problems I cause them. Long before I had a child of my own, I asked my mother if all the things she did for me cost her anything. After all, she loved me; didn't she freely choose to do all this for me? She just looked at me and laughed.

The air-conditioning in my son's car died. The only place that can repair it is about thirty-five miles from the town in which we live. My son and his wife both work full-time and can't get the car to the repair shop. I volunteer to do that for them. It will take up most of my day, yet I'm willing to do it. Do I want to do it? No, but I feel obligated to do it. Are they causing me problems? Yes. Will my son add this to his *Naikan* list of "Problems I Caused My Dad"? If he doesn't, I will.

So where does *Naikan* leave you? Guilty? Perhaps. Humbled? Absolutely. Grateful? Ah, yes, grateful—very, very, grateful. And motivated. The genius of *Naikan* is that once you realize just how gifted you are by life, you naturally turn to gifting other lives. As Krech explains:

> We often live our lives as if the world owes us. "Why didn't I get that raise?" "Why is the pizza so late?" "How come I don't get more appreciation from my boss?" We resent it when people do not fulfill our expectations, living as if we deserve whatever we want. When people do support us, we often take their efforts for granted, living as if we were entitled to such efforts. As we reflect on

our life we begin to see the reality of our life. What is more appropriate: to go through life with the mission of collecting what is owed us, or to go through life trying to repay our debt to others?[2]

When you play God, you seek to collect what you imagine is owed you. Living the surrendered life, you continually repay the debts you owe.

"For me, the greatest challenge in working the steps is making amends. Once I'd become clean I felt that the person I was is no longer the person I am, so why do I have to go back and clean up the messes that other me made? But eventually I realized that making amends was a way to repay debts I owed to people. Having stolen their trust in me, I was now—in some small way—returning it."

PAY IT FORWARD

You can't, of course, "pay back" the innumerable gifts you receive. As a spokesperson for AA wrote decades ago, "You can't pay anyone back for what has happened to you, so you try to find someone you can pay forward."[3]

The phrase "pay it forward" was coined by Lily Hardy Hammond in her novel *In the Garden of Delight*, and I am partial to Ralph Waldo Emerson's expression of the idea: "In the order of nature we cannot render benefits to those from whom we receive them, or only seldom. But the benefit we receive must be rendered again, line for line, deed for deed, cent for cent, to somebody."[4]

Paying it forward is not limited to the gifts you receive from your fellow humans and animals. It also includes the gifts you receive from inanimate objects. David Reynolds was my first *Naikan* teacher and the first to bring *Naikan* to the West. During one ten-day *Naikan* training retreat, he would meet with participants privately to assess their understanding of *Naikan*. One morning he asked to meet with me privately in the kitchen. As I entered the room I noticed that the faucet of the sink was dripping water. Before sitting down, I walked to the sink and closed the valve. "Why did you do that?" David asked. "To thank the sink for bringing water into the kitchen," I said. "The meeting is over," he said.

There are many good reasons to stop a sink from dripping: wasting water is wrong, and the sound of dripping water is distracting and annoying to name only two. But the *Naikan* reason is to thank the sink by assisting it in doing its task as well as it can be done. The fourteenth-century Christian mystic Meister Eckhart is quoted as saying, "If the only prayer you say in your entire life is 'thank you,' it is enough." Gregg Krech explains why:

> The best reason I can offer for saying thank you to socks [and other inanimate objects] is that they deserve it. Doesn't anything that serves, supports, and cares for us deserve a word of thanks? But here's another reason. Saying thank you to people and things will change your experience of life. Each moment we say thanks is a shift in our attention. A shift away from our self-centeredness toward others. A shift away from our problems and difficulties toward the support we are receiving from the world. Our attention is our life. Shifting our attention opens us to reality and reveals what has been there all along: socks.[5]

As gratitude deepens in your life it becomes more than a feeling; it becomes a life stance, the way you encounter and understand reality. Gratitude arises from inter-being and fuels the I-Thou understanding of life. As it does you discover that as much as you are here to serve life, life seems to be serving you even more.

THE FALLACY OF SELF-RELIANCE

"I hate feeling grateful," a young woman in an Al-Anon meeting said. "At least I hate feeling grateful to people. It makes me feel guilty. I mean, they went out of their way to help me, and I can't reciprocate, so I feel bad. I feel guilty and I have enough guilt in my life already. Then I start to think that they expect me to repay their help in some way, and, since I can't, they must be thinking poorly of me. Then the guilt shifts to shame, and sometimes the shame shifts to anger, and I avoid having contact with the person who helped me. So, really, I'd rather not be beholden to anyone."

To be beholden is to be indebted and morally obligated to another. I can see why someone might not like this idea. We want to be free to do what we want to do without having to take the needs and feelings of others into account. But what we want and what is real may be two different things. Unless you live alone, completely isolated from others and the products of their hands, you are beholden.

"That's why I love Henry David Thoreau," a young man explained to me. "While I'm not strong enough to do it, I love the idea of Thoreau abandoning civilization and living in a cabin of his own construction in the wilderness of Walden Pond. Being alone, being on your own, testing yourself against nature—it sounds wonderful. But I'm not man enough to actually do it." Neither was Thoreau.

Here is what Thoreau said he was doing: "I went to the woods because I wished to live deliberately, to confront only the essential facts of life, and see if I could not learn what it had to teach, and not, when I came to die, discover that I had not lived. . . . I wanted to live deep and suck out all the marrow of life."[6]

I remember how stirring this passage was the first few times I read it. Like the young man who reminded me of it, I too felt inadequate to this challenge. Then I learned that Thoreau was as well. First, his woods were owned by his friend Ralph Waldo Emerson. He was camping out in Emerson's backyard. Second, he dropped his laundry off at his mother's for her to wash. Third, he was close enough to town to walk in regularly and maintain social contacts. Fourth, he spent a lot of his time reading books someone else wrote, printed, bound, shipped, and sold.

Imagine our hero dropping off his laundry at his mom's house. He walks in the front door while his mother is out back tending her garden: "Henry? Henry, is that you?" "Yeah, Ma, its me." "What are you doing?" "Sucking the marrow out of life, Ma, just like last week. I'm leaving my laundry. And remember to tie up the clean stuff with some twine this time. It makes it easier to carry back to Ralph's place." "Sure, Henry. Can you stay a while and talk?" "Sorry, Ma, but I gotta walk into town to talk to some fellas about what it's like living on my own." "That's nice, dear. I left lunch for you on the kitchen table. No bones to suck the marrow out of, but a nice cheese sandwich all the same. You go talk with your friends while I do your laundry." "Thanks, Ma. I'll pick it up tomorrow."

My point isn't to disrespect Thoreau but to make it clear that we are too entangled in the web of life to imagine we can be completely self-reliant.

Gratitude is a life stance, and since all life is a verb, gratitude is also an action. Just as you are being gifted by life, so you must gift others in return. This isn't a commandment to which you must acquiesce; it is a natural consequence of your knowing how life really is.

To live a life of gratitude is to live a life that continually honors the gifts you receive by gifting others with gifts of your own.

FORGIVENESS

Some people store grudges the way others store recipes. My wife's grandmother used to keep tin file boxes crammed with recipes: some neatly folded and others crushed and bent; some carefully printed out by hand in pen or pencil; others cut from magazines or torn from newspapers now yellowed with age. There seemed to be no order to her collection of recipes, though whenever she needed a specific recipe she knew exactly where to find it. Today's grandmothers may do something similar using a computer, smartphone, or tablet, and while the filing system may have changed, the passion for collecting, stuffing, and storing has not.

It is the same with grudges, slights, past hurts, and painful memories. While you may not keep them in tin file boxes or on digital flash drives, you most likely cram them into your brain's memory banks where, like grandmother's recipes, they are easily retrieved when needed. When do you need them? Whenever you want to feel a bit holier-than-thou, cede to yourself the moral high ground, or justify your recurring anger at someone or another.

Lest you think I'm not talking about you, try this little experiment: Take a moment and think back to the earliest memory you have of being hurt by someone you trusted, liked, or loved. If you are like most people, such memories are not difficult to recall.

For example, as soon as I ask myself this question, I remember a "friend" in the seventh grade who would back me against a wall and wail into my stomach with his fists clenched almost as tightly as his jaw. He was a good twelve inches shorter than me, and nowhere near my weight. I never hit him back, but I would look down on him and say, "What the hell do you think you're doing?" After throwing a few more punches he would realize that he wasn't hurting me, and he would stop the pounding. I doubt he had a clue as to why he exploded this way or why I was his preferred target. I just kept the pounds on to protect myself from the pounding. Did I ever forgive him for his bullying? No.

Forgiveness isn't the end of hurt or the possibility of being hurt. It is simply moving on a bit more wisely. Forgiveness won't erase the past, but it just might free you from it; it won't save you from suffering, but it just might help you realize that suffering is simply part of the human condition, and thus allow you to suffer without the added element of surprise. Maybe forgiveness is simply the stripping away of illusion so that you can navigate your way through life with more clarity and less bruising.

"I sometimes think I've never actually forgiven anyone in my entire life. I'm not even sure I know what forgiveness is. Is it forgetting what was done to me, or excusing what was done to me, or simply accepting what was done to me? All this seems like a waste of time. Stuff happens. Move on. Forgiveness is beside the point."

WHAT IT IS, WHAT IT'S NOT

Most talk about forgiveness assumes forgiveness is a skill you can learn and use whenever you wish. I disagree. Forgiveness isn't a skill, but a level of understanding of the nature of life and how best to live it. It isn't something you can use the way you might use an umbrella or a fork. It is an understanding of self and others and life in general that can be cultivated rather than something that can be mastered.

Some say forgiveness is a way to escape suffering. I don't. Forgiveness isn't a tactic you can employ to make your life less stressful. Forgiveness isn't something you can deploy to end suffering. Suffering is a part of life. The Buddha went so far as to say that suffering is life, or at least life is suffering when you continue to live it in a manner rooted in craving, grasping, and playing God, and the anger, arrogance, and jealousy that erupts from craving, grasping, and playing God.

I don't think you can escape suffering, nor should you try. Life is what it is: ten thousand joys and ten thousand sorrows. Forgiveness won't change that. But it can free you from dragging sorrow into your moments of joy, and that is no small thing at all.

NO CURE FOR CONFLICT

Life without conflict is no life at all.

What causes conflict? It's simple: you have a plan and nothing goes according to it. Now what do you do? You are dating the partner of a lifetime only to find out you've been double-timed. You land the job of your dreams and your boss turns out to be an abusive SOB. Or your best friend gets cancer and dies. Or your parent abandons you. Or your sibling commits suicide. Or any number of horrible things that can happen to people happens to you. Now what do you do?

You might imagine that you would prefer a life without conflict. But without conflict you can't grow or develop character; without conflict you would find life boring and meaningless. Recovering and being surrendered doesn't bring an end to conflict. It simply brings an end to the desire to bring an end to conflict.

"Before entering OA I thought addictive eating was the source of all the conflict in my life. Then I cleaned up my eating, but conflicts continued. Then I thought working the steps over and over would bring an end to conflicts, but that too proved wrong. I now think my addiction masked conflict and eating sane uncovers them and forces me to deal with them."

Conflict is natural to life and imagining you can escape it is nonsense. Conflict is systemic to life, which means that hurting and being hurt are also part of the way things are. No amount of forgiveness will erase this. Forgiveness is not a one-time act but an ongoing attitude rooted in the realization that conflict is as natural to living as breathing.

THE MESS OF THE QUEST

When I think of people who have hurt me I discover something interesting. The people who hurt me the most are people I love the most. I'm not saying that these are people I loved in the past and whom I cease to love when they cause me to suffer, but rather the people who caused me to suffer in the past are often people I still love in the present. I don't love them because they hurt me; I'm not a masochist. Nor do I love them in spite of their hurting me; I'm not a saint. I just still love them. When I think about those moments when they hurt me, I discover through that love something else: they didn't have a choice.

When people hurt you, chances are you imagine they could have done otherwise. In fact, if you don't assume this, you wouldn't have the moral high ground from which to be hurt and bestow forgiveness. But is this true? Can people do other than they do?

I think people are simple: you want to be happy and will do lots of stupid things to make yourself happy. Most of these things don't work and leave you with messes to clean up. Sometimes you act like an adult and clean up those messes. Most often you act like a child and leave them for someone else to clean up. But rarely do you set out to make a mess. You set out to be happy, and it is the quest for happiness that makes the mess.

"It wasn't hard for me to admit that my life had become unmanageable. What was hard was admitting I was unmanageable. And what was harder still was admitting that other people and situations were unmanageable."

"My sponsor told me once, he said, "When you drink you are like a bull in a china shop raging around and making a huge mess. When you sober up you are still a bull in a china shop raging around and making a mess, but the new china shop is more luxurious than the older one.""

Think of the last three times you hurt people. Write down what you did and why it caused another to suffer. Now write down your motive for doing what you did. Be honest: Did you deliberately set out to hurt the other person? Or were you pursuing some other goal, some personal happiness or pleasure, and the person you hurt was collateral damage?

Most people don't set out to deliberately hurt you. Most people aren't sociopaths. Most people get caught up in the pursuit of happiness and are as surprised as you are when their pursuit causes you pain. Should you abandon your pursuit of happiness and instead set out to make yourself miserable? No, that wouldn't change things much. You would just make different messes and always for the same reason: you set out in pursuit of something.

When you set out to make yourself happy (or miserable if you prefer), you must control those around you. You must script a play and convince or force others to play the parts you have written for them. In other words, you must play God. This rarely works. People refuse to read their lines or take their places or let you have your way. They have their own scripts from which they want you to read, and they have committed themselves to their own preferred outcomes. It's just a mess. But there is an alternative: stop trying to script your life and just go about living it.

What does it mean to just live your life? Am I suggesting you have no plan, no dream, and no preferences as to what happens to you and those you love? Not at all. Planning, dreaming, and having preferences are natural, and they are no more yours to control than the actions of those you love. Even as you plan, dream, and desire this over that, just remind yourself that you have no control over any of it.

DEBUNKING THE LAW OF ATTRACTION

"That is simply a matter of defeatist thinking," a middle-aged woman wearing a "Think and Grow Rich" T-shirt said when I shared my notion that you lack control over your life. "If you think you have no control then you won't have control. But if you think you do have control, you will. This is the Law of Attraction built into the fabric of the universe: your thoughts create your reality. Think rich, grow rich; think healthy, be healthy. You have absolute control. Everything that happens to you happens because you will it to happen, because your thoughts attract it into your life."

The law of attraction is the notion that like attracts like. As Rhonda Byrne, author of *The Secret*, writes:

> You are the most powerful magnet in the Universe! You contain a magnetic power within you that is more powerful than anything in this world, and this unfathomable magnetic power is emitted through your thoughts.... The law of attraction says *like attracts like*, and so as you think a thought, you are also attracting *like* thoughts to you.[1]

"I never argue with people who say they are magnets," Burt said. "I only point out that the law of magnetic attraction is the exact opposite of what they say it is. The truth about magnets is that opposites attract, and like repels like. Insisting you can change the very laws of physics just by willing it so is playing God on steroids."

I've read *The Secret* and watched the movie, and I understand the notion that my thoughts create my future: think good, get good; think bad, get bad. I'm not saying this is true—in fact, it is false—but it sounds good because it restores your sense of mastery over life. If I control my thinking, I will "manifest" the world I want. Great. At least it sounds great until I realize that most of my thinking happens in my subconscious mind beyond the control of my conscious me.

According to the *think good, get good* theory, the universe responds to your thoughts and does your bidding; the trick is to avoid thinking negative thoughts. The problem is that by the time you know you're thinking negatively, you have already thought negatively and the universe is gearing up to dump a whole lot of negative on you. Even if you quickly shift gears and try to ward off the negative with lots of positive, the thought that you are doing this to stave off the negative actually causes the universe to heap even more negativity on you. You're doomed!

Rather than seek to control the universe, why not learn to navigate it instead?

WHO'S IN CHARGE HERE?

As we said early on, you can't control your thoughts. You can, for a time, deliberately think about one thing or another, but you cannot avoid thoughts you don't want to think. Furthermore, you don't even know you have unwanted thoughts until you have already thought them. Go ahead, make a mental list of all the thoughts you don't want to think. Uh-oh. You've just thought each of them!

Now I'm not the first person to realize this. In fact, *The Secret* makes the same point. The solution, we are told, is to focus on feelings. You can tell how you are thinking by how you are feeling, and you can control your thinking by controlling your feelings.[2] Forget *think good, get good* and focus on *feel good, get good* instead. Unfortunately, this doesn't help at all because you can no more control your feelings than you can control your thoughts.

If you could control your feelings, you wouldn't ever feel sad, angry, fearful, or envious. You'd just feel happy all the time. But you don't feel happy all the time. Insisting you can and should is just setting yourself up for more failure and, hence, greater negativity.

You can't control your feelings for the same reason you can't control your thoughts: feelings rise of their own accord without your conscious mind deciding one way or another. By the time your conscious mind knows what you're feeling, you're already feeling it. Your only choice is what to do with your thoughts and feelings once they are thought and felt, not whether or not to think or feel them in the first place. Even this is problematic.

Point your right index finger at your nose. Whenever you feel like it, and completely at your own command, point that finger at your stomach instead. Whether you did this exercise or not, you made a decision: "I'm going to point my finger at my nose and shift it to my stomach, or I'm not. My choice." But is it? When you engage in some voluntary action, the prefrontal region of your brain sends messages to the premotor cortex, which in turn sends messages to the primary motor cortex, which in turn sends out the command to move your finger. But who initiates this? As Burt never tired of reminding me, "It ain't you, babe."

IT AIN'T "ME" BABE

In 1985, Benjamin Libet, a researcher at the University of California in San Francisco, discovered that your brain prepared to move your finger one-third of a second prior to your conscious decision to move your finger. So did you consciously decide to move your finger or did you simply acquiesce to what was already happening in your brain?

You may not accept Libet's findings. Accepting them seems to suggest that you are not in control, that you are not the boss of your own body and mind, and this can be troubling. After all, if you aren't in control of "me," who is? The answer I prefer is this: no one. That subjective experience I call "me" isn't independent of my physical sensations, emotions, and thoughts. It is an epiphenomenon that becomes conscious of them after the fact. I don't think my thoughts; my thoughts somehow think me.

I realize we have gone through this before, and I'm raising this issue again in the context of forgiveness to make the following point: you aren't really in control of what you think, feel, and do, and neither is anyone else. If no one is doing anything "on purpose," how can you weave your epic tales of woe that make forgiveness so important in the first place?

When you know you can't control your thoughts and feelings, you stop blaming yourself for what you think and feel, and you stop insisting that other people control their thoughts and feelings as well. When you stop insisting that other people control their thoughts and feelings, you stop expecting them to think and feel the way you do, or the way you wish them to think and feel. You simply expect them to think and feel, and to be as surprised and humbled by their thoughts and feelings as you are by your own, though this, too, is outside your control.

"When I was high I would think the most amazing thoughts. I was convinced I was a genius. Then I'd come down and think how stupid these thoughts were and how stupid I am. When I got off the drugs I found I still thought amazing and amazingly stupid thoughts, but now I no longer blame myself for thinking them."

All this is freeing. Knowing that thoughts and feelings just happen allows you to just think and feel without judging anyone, yourself included. To paraphrase Jesus, "Let those without out a crazy thought cast the first stone."

LIFE IS WILD

Forgiveness arises naturally once you are surrendered to the fundamental wildness of life. When you see that life is neither controlled nor controllable, that what is rarely conforms precisely to your assessment of what should be, all arrogance dissipates. You stop insisting that life be other than it is, or that people be other than they are. You realize that we are all working within the confines of our conditioning—genetic, parental, religious, societal, and so forth. And with this realization comes the greater surrender to the Power Greater than your conditioned self, the Power that arises in you as the unconditioned and unconditional I'ing.

"When we talk about forgiveness in its truest form," Burt explained, "we aren't talking about me, the conditioned self, but about the unconditioned surrendered self. Take racism, misogyny, ethnic hatreds, the hatred of Jews or Muslims. People aren't born racists; they are taught to be racists, they are conditioned to be racists. A 'me' who defines him or herself as racist can't simply stop being a racist even if you outlaw racism: their conditioning is too strong. They can only stop being a racist when they stop being "me." Twelve-Step spirituality and all authentic spiritual practice isn't about making a better me; it's all about ceasing to be me altogether."

Forgiveness happens naturally when you cease to be "me" and stop playing God, and realize I'ing as your truest self. But forgiving others isn't the same as endorsing them or excusing what they do. Nor does it mean that people engaging in evil shouldn't be punished or imprisoned, or that you should maintain a relationship with people no matter what they do to you, or that you should acquiesce to societal evil or injustice. It only means that you realize that all this evil is the result of conditions over which the conditioned self has no control. The promise of Twelve-Step spirituality, as evidenced in the first three steps, isn't the capacity to control or end our conditioning, but to no longer be the conditioned "me" in the first place.

"I know lots of people who shun me because of the hurt
I caused them when I was drinking. It doesn't matter
to them that I'm no longer drinking and no longer the

person I was when I was drinking. It doesn't matter
that I've made amends or tried to make amends. But it
matters to me. The gift of the Twelve Steps is not a better
me but a new me."

Burt said, "When life is painful, the surrendered self feels
pain. When life is joyous, the surrendered self feels joy. When
harm is done, the surrendered self makes amends. When
harm is received, the surrendered self forgives. This is what it
is to be surrendered: living in tune with the moment. When
the moment changes, as it always does, the surrendered self
changes along with it."

When you understand the nature of reality you expect
to be hurt. Not all the time and not by everyone, but often
enough by those you love that it isn't a shock—even when it
may still be a surprise. You expect to be hurt not because you
think people are mean and hurtful but because you know that
people are most often victims of their own inner turmoil, and
this turmoil just erupts now and again in ways that hurt you.

"This is what I know: we are all bozos on this bus; we all
screw up; we all flounder around; we all do the best we
can even when the best of one moment is seen as the
worst a moment later. Nothing makes sense and yet we
try to make sense out of it anyway. That's why Christ says,
'Forgive them, Father, for they know not what they do.'
Nobody knows, not even Father. Forgiveness is just what
we do when we realize nobody knows."

LIVING FORGIVENESS

If you insist people are free—absolutely free and therefore
absolutely responsible for what they think, feel, and do—you

will have a difficult time forgiving those who hurt you. But if you know that people who do evil are trapped in such a way as to make their actions anything but freely chosen, you can forgive them. But forgiving them is not the same as forgiving their behavior. You can have compassion for their inner turmoil and entrapment. But you don't have to let that compassion erase the danger this person represents. Forgiveness in this context is never-ending because screwing up is never-ending. "Peter approached Jesus and asked, 'Lord, if another sins against me, how often should I forgive? As many as seven times?' Jesus said to him, 'Not seven times, but, I tell you, seventy-seven times" (Matthew 18:21–22, NRSV). When you realize the truth of your nature, forgiveness happens.

"I used to think I had to seek forgiveness from people. Then I used to think I had to bestow forgiveness on people. Now I neither seek or bestow and forgiveness just happens. And the strangest discovery for me was that along with forgiveness came humility. In fact I'm pretty certain that forgiveness and humility are almost flip sides of the same awakening."

HUMILITY

As I noted earlier, it is common for us to refer to ourselves as recovering addicts, not as recovered addicts. I have heard some say that this choice of language is part of the cult of Twelve-Step: if we are only recovering and never recovered we can never leave the fold, never put the steps aside. I understand the criticism, and even admit that Twelve-Step meetings can become addictive. Just as we once preferred to drink, drug, overeat, gamble, and the like, rather than live our lives, some among us prefer to go to meetings rather than to live our lives. But this has nothing to do with the deeper meaning of "recovering" and has everything to do with humility.

"I haven't had a drink in twenty years. The chances of me going to a bar if I skipped a meeting are slim to none. If I abandoned meetings and working the steps altogether, however, I'd be back to drinking in no time. I'm not a new person. I'm not a different person. I'm not other than I was. I'm simply the person I was when I didn't drink. But the person I was when I did drink is still here as well. Knowing that keeps me coming back to meetings. Knowing that never allows me to say I'm a recovered

alcoholic, only a recovering one. Knowing that keeps me
humble, and humility keeps me sober."

As Bill W. tells us in *Twelve Steps and Twelve Traditions*,
"Humility, as a word and as an ideal, has a very bad time of
it in our world. Not only is the idea misunderstood; the word
itself is often intensely disliked. Many people haven't even a
nodding acquaintance with humility as a way of life."[1]

Humility is one of the great gifts of being surrendered.
Humility comes from the Latin *humilitas*, "being grounded or
from the earth (*humus*)." Being of the earth is your true nature:
you are of the earth in the same way a tree or plant is of the
earth. The Hebrew Bible makes the same point when it speaks
of *adam*, "earthling," from *adamah*, "earth." You are *adamah*
becoming *adam*, *humus* becoming human; earth becoming
earthling. You are nature becoming aware of herself; and your
task is "to till the garden and take care of it" (Genesis 2:15). In
other words, you come from the earth to care for the earth,
and you can only do this when you are close to the earth; that
is to say, when you are humble. And you are humbled when
you are surrendered to the Power Greater than Ourselves, the
I'ing that is the very nature of which you are a part.

"Here is what I know now: the more I'm humbled, the
more I stop playing God, the more I find myself in service
to others and to life as a whole, the more forgiveness
happens with me. I thought these were two separate
things, but they're not. Forgiveness and humility go
together like back goes with front."

Humility brings you back to your true nature. Coming
back to your true nature is regaining your sanity, coming to

your senses, living without the madness of addiction, and in service to life. Coming back to your true nature, the I'ing, makes forgiving simply a part of who you are.

COMING BACK TO WHAT'S TRUE

What keeps you from being humble and coming back to what is true is your focus on the illusion that you are other than *adamah*, other than the earth, other than a manifesting of reality and somehow the master of reality instead. In other words, what keeps you from realizing your true nature is your insistence on playing God.

"My toddler loves to dress up in superhero costumes. At first I feared that she would mistake herself for the superhero and forget who she really was. But every time I would ask her who she was she always answered 'Mia,' regardless of the costume she was wearing. As my understanding of the Twelves Steps deepened I came to see that my fear for Mia was a projection of my own reality. I too dressed up in a superhero costume. My costume was God. But unlike my daughter, I did forget who I truly was."

When you are intent on affirming yourself absolutely as a distinct being, as the twentieth-century French psychotherapist Hubert Benoit calls it, you are not humble. You aren't a servant of life but one who seeks to lord over life and especially over the lives of those who impact your own life. You are so caught up in the fantasy of playing God that you cannot see things as they are. The more you fail to see things as they are, the more special you imagine yourself to be. If you must admit to being powerless in Step One, your attitude is still narcissistic: "Look at me! Look at me! I'm so weak, so powerless, so beyond redemption that no matter what I do I cannot achieve liberation." Your impotence becomes proof of your own importance. Benoit explains:

> When the outside world is positive, constructive, it is as I want it, and it then appears to me as conditioned by me; when it is negative, destructive (even if that does not directly concern me), it is as I do not want it, and it appears to me then as refusing to let itself be conditioned by me.[2]

But when seen without the conceit of playing God, you see that your entire experience of reality is conditioned by your likes and dislikes. You discover that you live at the mercy of your preferences and imagine a God—the God of your understanding—who shares your preferences.

"I was never more important than when I drank. I mean, I drank not by choice but out of necessity. It was the way I coped with being unimportant. I know this sounds paradoxical, but the way I see it now is that when I wasn't drinking I wanted to be important, but I wasn't. When I drank, I felt like the least capable person in the world— nobody was more of a drunk than me; nobody was more of a loser than me. You get it? I was the best drunk! If I couldn't be the center of the sober world, I would be the center of the alcoholic world."

GET LOW

When surrendered to reality and humbled by it, you live without this pretense and the God who maintains it. Because you no longer expect the universe to conform to your will, you aren't distressed when the universe doesn't conform to your will. Like the Monk Begging for Food, you stand with arms stretched out and hands open to accept the ten thousand joys and ten thousand sorrows, the birthing and dying and blessing and cursing that is life as we humans experience it. It isn't that you are passive in the face of what is but that you no longer resist what is. When you no longer resist what is, you can work with it and within it to tend the garden as best you can.

This is what Jesus meant us to understand when he said the meek shall inherit the earth, (Matthew 5:5). To be meek isn't to be passive but to be humbled, to be lowered down. Jesus took his teaching from Psalm 37:11, "The humble shall inherit the earth, and delight in abundant peace."

Burt said, "Christ is a Christian, Jesus is a Taoist. Being humble is being low, seeking the low is the way of water and water is representative of the way of Tao: 'The greatest good follows the way of water benefitting all things even as it occupies the low places people disparage. In this it is near to Tao' (Tao Te Ching 8). Water always flows to the lowest point. The humble reside at that lowest point, and because they do, all things come to them: the good and the bad, the blessings and the cursings. This is what it is to inherit the earth"

Inheriting the earth has nothing to do with ruling the earth but rather being open to and receiving things as they are. Your task is to tend the garden: to engage with whatever comes in such a way as to place it and yourself in service to life. Whether good or bad, whether something you desire or something you despise, your challenge is to place what is in service to life's flourishing. Life's flourishing, not your flourishing. You are the servant and not the master. The Bible calls this being "a blessing to all the families of the earth" (Genesis 12:3). "All the families," human and otherwise.

Benoit teaches, "In our desire to escape from distress at last, we search for doctrines of salvation, we search for 'gurus'.

But the true guru is not far away, he is before your eyes and unceasingly offers us his teaching; he is reality as it is, he is our daily life."[3]

"I loved playing God. Then I discovered I was God and the playing stopped. Everything became so serious, and I felt immobilized. Then I discovered that God was me and all seriousness fell away and the play resumed, but my part had changed. I was no longer playing God, but God was playing me and you and everybody. The joy in this play dwarfs the pleasure I got from playing God."

To be humbled is to be grounded. To be grounded is to hit rock bottom and experience the shattering of "me" that plays God. It is the shattering of I-It and the liberation of I-Thou, but only for a while. You are never recovered, only recovering, and this means that if the conditions are ripe, I-It will again surface and resume playing God. But the more aware you are of the way the game is played, the more open you are to having "me" shattered once again. There is no final shattering, no absolute rock bottom, no ultimate liberation; only another shattering, another rock bottom, another liberation.

"I've been clean several times. Each time I am, I see the madness of using, and I promise not to use drugs again. I'm sincere. I mean it every time I say it, but things change and I stop seeing so clearly, and this voice in my head keeps telling me that I'd be happier using again, but that isn't really what gets me using. I turn to drugs the same way I turn to recovery—I can't do anything else. At least that's what I used to say, but it isn't really true. I was pretending to be powerless over drugs. The truth was I turned to drugs to gain power over what I was really powerless over—life. When I realize that I'm truly powerless over life, I no longer seek to gain power, and the pull of the drug is so much less enticing. I'm not saying I won't use again, I'm only saying that right now, knowing what I know, doing so seems a distant possibility."

HUMILITY IS NOT A GOAL

Be careful not to make humility a goal or self–humbling a way toward a goal. Doing so only feeds "me" and its pretense to power. Rather than strive to be somebody, you will strive to be nobody. Rather than struggle to have something, you will struggle to have little and judge yourself negatively against those who seem to have even less. All you need do is see what is true in this and every moment and allow striving and struggle to diminish in the light of what you see.

Burt used to say, "Don't imagine you can live without negative thoughts and feelings, or without striving and struggling. Imagining this only sets you up for the delusion of control. Rather know that once surrendered from the need to control, you are free from being controlled. Crazy thoughts and feelings still arise, but you're no longer obligated to deal with them. The urge to strive after and struggle for control subsides; it is more a ripple than a tidal wave. That is the freedom recovery promises."

The other day I watched a documentary on the history of donuts. I haven't eaten a donut in over thirty years, but there was no denying that when the camera zeroed in on a basket of freshly baked chocolate glazed donuts, my entire body went into craving mode. "I want that," I said to myself. "Who wouldn't?" I replied. "Do you remember how amazing they taste?" "Yep. Especially with a glass of cold milk." The conversation continued for a couple of minutes. I didn't do anything to stop it. I didn't try and change anything. I simply noticed what was happening. No aversion, no affection; just attention. After thirty plus years without a donut, I watched as the desire to eat one—who am I kidding; the desire to each six—arose as strongly as ever. You'd think it would have weakened by now, but that wasn't my experience. My desire hadn't changed. What changed was my desire to acquiesce to or resist that desire. This is what it is to be humbled. This is what it is to live surrendered.

THERE IS NOTHING YOU CAN DO, AND ONLY YOU CAN DO IT

Many years ago, after a decade of daily *zazen*, Zen meditation practice, I called my teacher Taitetsu Unno to complain that I had yet to achieve enlightenment. While he once told me that he preferred to leave his enlightenment to a future incarnation, I, not being a believer in reincarnation, was in something of a hurry. Professor Unno was both a Pure Land Buddhist priest and a serious student of Zen. After listening to my concerns, he invited me to speak with him in person. I flew from my home in Miami, Florida, visited a bit with my family in Springfield, Massachusetts, and drove the twenty-three miles to meet with him at Smith College in Northampton.

Zen Buddhism is firmly rooted in *jiriki*, self-power. Your enlightenment is in your hands and your hands alone. This is where I was coming from: it is all about self-power. Pure Land Buddhism is firmly rooted in *tariki*, other-power. Your enlightenment comes through the grace of Amitabha Buddha, the Buddha of Infinite Light. You cannot achieve enlightenment on your own but only by calling upon Amitabha Buddha to do it for you. Professor Unno was of both schools, and said to me, "There is nothing you can do, and only you can do it."

You might think me crazy to fly all the way from Miami, Florida, for this bit of "fortune cookie wisdom," as several friends called it, but sitting across from my beloved teacher and receiving this teaching face-to-face (*menju*, in Japanese) was revelatory to me. It changed everything and reminded me of a teaching from my own tradition: "You are not obligated to complete the task [of healing the world], nor are you free to abandon it" (*Pirkei Avot* 2:21). "Just so," Professor Unno said when I shared this teaching with him.

As I prepared to drive back to my parents' house, Professor Unno suggested I study the *Xinxin Ming*, "Truthful Mind," a poem attributed to the contemporary Buddhist monk and religious scholar Sheng-Yen, the Third Patriarch of Ch'an (Zen) Buddhism. While written as a self-power rebuttal to the other-power teachings of Pure Land Buddhism, Professor Unno invited me to read *Xinxin Ming* as a bridge uniting *jiriki* (self-power) and *tariki* (other-power). I had intended to translate the text myself and send him the finished version for commentary. I never did. Remembering this long-forgotten promise, I am paying forward my debt to my now deceased teacher by "translating" the *Xinxin Ming* in the context of recovery and sharing it with you as way of summarizing all we have said in this book.

> *The true Way isn't difficult:*
> *Just abandon liking and disliking and*
> *Freedom happens of its own accord.*

When you see the way "me" likes and dislikes; when you realize that liking and disliking are not under your control but rather the result of the conditioning you received from both nature and nurture, you no longer cling to liking and disliking. No longer clinging to liking and disliking, you no longer pursue the former or seek to escape the latter. With nothing to chase after or run away from, you are free.

> *Escaping addiction*
> *Makes addiction stronger.*
> *Pursuing recovery*
> *Makes recovery elusive.*
> *Liking/disliking, escaping/pursuing*
> *This is your real disease.*
> *If you don't understand this,*
> *Nothing you do will free you.*
> *If you do understand this*
> *You are already free.*

The key is understanding: not the understanding that comes from study or disciplined spiritual practice but the understanding that comes simply from observing what is of itself so. Do you have to study water to know it is wet? Or do you simply experience water and get wet?

> *Chasing stillness*
> *You only make more waves.*
> *Caught between action and non-action,*
> *Surrender and being surrendered,*
> *You cannot know yourself as the One, and*
> *Hence become forever mesmerized by the two.*

Being surrendered happens when the conditions for being surrendered are such that nothing else can happen. The conditions for being surrendered arise only when you have exhausted all efforts at surrendering. Twelve-Step spirituality, like so many authentic spiritual practices, is designed to exhaust you, to strip you of *jiriki*, self-power, and the illusion you are in control.

The One is a boundless ocean.
The ten thousand things are its waves.
Clinging to the former
There is no love.
Clinging to the latter
There is no awe.
Understanding both
You welcome all and resist nothing.

Holding to the ocean, you are caught in the idea of recovery. Holding to the waves, you are caught in the idea of addiction. Understanding both, you effortlessly ride the surf of recovering. The more you desire to be free from addiction, the more you tighten the grip of addiction. The more you try to surrender, the more trapped you become in the illusion of control. Only when you are surrendered of the idea of recovery are you free from your self-powered will for surrender. Once you are free, sobriety is your only reality.

The more you crave sobriety
The more addicted you become.
Give up "drunk" and "sober"
And all obstacles disappear.
The moment you dwell on "drunk" and "sober"
All truth is lost.

Words are not value-free. They carry weight; they convey judgment. If you despise yourself for being addicted, you make the addicted self the center of your reality. If you place sobriety on a pedestal, you make your sober self the center of your reality. In either case, you—the "me" you imagine yourself to be—are the center, and it is the illusion of being the center that is root cause of your disease.

When there is nothing wrong
Addiction and recovery are irrelevant.
When addiction and recovery are irrelevant
Addict and recovering addict fade away.
When addict and recovering addict fade away
There is just the Happening of all happening
happening as you.

You might worry that if addiction and recovery are both irrelevant you will continue with your addiction. But thinking this way assumes that your addiction is relevant. When something is completely irrelevant to you, you have nothing to do with it. It is immaterial to you and no longer connected with you. And when addiction is no longer related to you, recovery too becomes irrelevant.

Do not reject what repulses you.
Do not embrace what attracts you.
Be present with each and see the interbeing of both.

When you are simply present to disliking and liking without judgment, and you know that both arise of their own accord, there is no need to act upon either. You needn't distance yourself from one or draw near to the other. You needn't avoid what is arising in any way or label what arises as "disliking" or "liking," "repulsion" or "attraction," as if labeling will weaken their hold on you. You needn't become the witness or the observer of your thoughts and feelings. You need only be present. Being present is the stance of the Monk Begging for Food: it is just you open to what is rather than hiding from what is.

Pursuing recovery only fosters addiction.
Caught between addiction and recovery,
Narrow mind obsesses over playing God.

You engage in the Twelve Steps for their own sake. If you have no ulterior motive, if you don't work the steps to change yourself or your situation but only do them because doing them seems right, you are free from results and can engage each step without coercion.

> *Caught between addiction and recovery*
> *You race after images of perfection*
> *And away from images of imperfection.*
> *The moment you do, all hope is lost.*

Perfection is no less a trap than imperfection. Both are fantasies of your own creation acting as blinders to seeing reality as it is. Pursuing perfection as you understand perfection only strengthens imperfection as you understand imperfection. Free from both, you are surrendered to what is and what is the sublime melancholy of *wabi-sabi*.

> *There is no need to seek the truth;*
> *The truth cannot be anywhere other than here.*
> *The truth of your addiction.*
> *The truth of your recovery.*
> *The truth of narrow mind.*
> *The truth of spacious mind.*
> *It is all here, only you are missing.*

J. Krishnamurti tells us, "Truth is a pathless land." Every path is away from here, while here is where truth resides. Truth is nothing other than the ten thousand joys and ten thousand sorrows of everyday existence. If you hope to escape this by seeking truth, the truth you seek is not true.

> *Dwell on nothing.*
> *Pursue nothing.*
> *Let your cravings crave.*
> *If you cease to scratch an itch,*
> *In time the itching stops.*

Being surrendered is being with what is without resisting, evading, judging, or yielding. If your addiction is triggered, your addiction is triggered. If your addiction is quiet, your addiction is quiet. It is all the same to you when you know that moments of addiction and moments of sobriety are just the way reality is reality.

> *No one can save you from your addiction,*
> *Including yourself.*
> *Do not climb the Steps one to twelve,*
> *Tumble down them one to twelve.*
> *Gravity rather than will is the better guru.*

You don't surrender yourself to gravity, you are surrendered to gravity. You don't will yourself to fall, you simply fall. You can fight gravity if you like, but you will never win that fight. Don't imagine you are fighting your addiction when you strive to be clean; know instead that what you are fighting is your recovery.

> *Do not reject narrow mind,*
> *Only come to understand it.*
> *Do not seek refuge in spacious mind,*
> *Only come to fathom it.*
> *Do not pit the one against the other,*
> *But know them both as "me."*

You aren't this or that, you are this and that. You aren't one way or another, you are one way and another. You are what you are according to the conditions at hand. You arise out of these, and you are never separate from them.

> *When you know the narrow and the spacious,*
> *Nothing is alien to you.*
> *When you no longer like the one or dislike the other*
> *Nothing frightens you.*

When you no longer fear your addiction, you aren't afraid of being an addict. When you aren't afraid of being an addict, you are no longer attached to the idea of recovery. When there is no fear of addiction or attachment to recovery, you are free, and free from both. You are a recovering addict through no effort of your own.

> *When likes and dislikes are no more*
> *Nothing is the same:*
> *There is no willful action yet all is done;*
> *There is no willful inaction yet all is at rest.*

This is *wei-wu-wei*, non-coercive action: going with the flow, cutting with the grain, saying "yes, and" to whatever arises, acting and not acting in tune with the conditions of the moment. This isn't addiction or recovery. This is recovering. This is being surrendered.

> *With doing and non-doing put aside*
> *Doubt fades and serenity reigns.*
> *Nothing is left out*
> *And nothing remains:*
> *Rising and falling—your simple reality.*

Living the surrendered life, living the recovering life, is just being with what is: the rising and falling of the ten thousand joys and ten thousand sorrows. You are not other than this; you are not better than this; you are not worse that this; you are this. And that is just fine.

> *Self-power, other-power—just talk.*
> *Do what you can and*
> *What you can't will happen on its own.*

All you can do is all you can do. When you do all you can do, the doing continues without you doing it. This is being surrendered. This is the gift of Twelve-Step spirituality. Not that you have accomplished something, and certainly not that you have accomplished something once and for all, but that you have done all you can do and then have been surrendered to the doing you cannot do at all.

> *Words fail.*
> *Practice stumbles.*
> *Thinking entraps.*
> *Feeling ensnares.*
> *The past fades.*
> *The future no longer unfurls.*
> *And the present too is no longer.*
> *There is no more concern with addiction and recovery;*
> *There is no more worry about finding Truth—*
> *You are Truth,*
> *And addiction and recovery take care of themselves.*

Just so.

INVITATIONS

Self-help books come with exercises to help you help yourself achieve whatever the author of the book is trying to help you achieve. This is not a self-help book. You cannot achieve the surrendered life, you can only be surrendered to it, and there are no exercises for achieving the unachievable. Yet there are things you can do as long as you don't expect anything special from them. I call these invitations.

My sponsor Burt once said to me, "A practice is something you do to achieve a specific end. An invitation is simply offering that end an opening. In other words, when I invite someone to a party I don't coerce their attendance, I simply make room for them, should they show up."

Without putting too fine a point on this, I send out invitations to surrendered living daily. Sometimes surrendered living shows up, sometimes it doesn't. At first an unanswered invitation would annoy me, but today my concern with attendance has largely faded. I send out invitations because I find myself sending out invitations, and finding myself doing so brings me joy, regardless of the invitation's effect.

What follows are a few of the invitations I send simply for the joy of sending them. I don't work at spirituality, I play with it; I don't practice meditation, I just sit and watch my mind reveling in the madness it calls reality. I'm no longer interested in awakening or enlightenment or any particular state of consciousness. The things I do, the invitations I send, such as singing, silent sitting, passage meditation, and the rest, I do the same way I breathe or beat my heart or grow my hair; that is to say "I" don't do them at all. They just happen. I wake up in the morning and the recitation of memorized sacred texts happens; I sit down some time later and thoughts and feelings arise in my mind and I inquire, "Who is thinking? Who is feeling?" I can't say I do any of these things mindfully or with attention or intention. I don't do them at all; they simply do themselves.

Nevertheless, I have no problem sharing with you what happens with me. Just don't imagine that doing any of these things will secure a surrendered state. Explore these invitations simply for the fun of exploration. If one or another intrigues you, you might engage with it more deliberately for a time, but don't make a ritual out of it. If it happens, it happens; if it doesn't happen, something else will happen. Something else is always happening.

MONK BEGGING FOR FOOD

If there is a physical stance embodying the surrendered life it would be the qigong posture of Monk Begging for Food. In some sects of Buddhism, a monk's survival depends on the generosity of others. Once each day the monk visits neighbors and receives whatever food they offer. It is completely *tariki*, other-power: what they eat and how well they eat is, pun intended, out of their hands. I've been taught to take this stance each morning. Some mornings I do, and some I don't. But I do take the stance whenever I notice myself resisting what is in hopes of turning what is into what I want it to be.

Monk Begging for Food is a way to invite a shift from *jiriki*, self-power, to *tariki*, other-power. When you notice yourself taking the stance of self-power, shift to the stance of other-power and see if your mental state doesn't shift from clinging to preferences to opening to reality as it is.

Stand with your feet shoulder width apart, you knees comfortably bent. Keeping your upper arms against the sides of your body, bend your elbow and stretch out your arms as if you are carrying a tray of food on your up-turned palms. Gently tuck in your chin toward your chest and allow your eyes to softly gaze unfocused on the ground. Hold the posture and breathe until your body tells you it is time to stop. Then stop. Or, as one teacher advised me, hold it an extra minute because my body tends to give in a little too soon.

JUST SITTING

I once asked Burt to describe his meditation practice to me. "I haven't meditated in years," he said, "unless you count this very moment." What he meant was this: formal meditation— rules and regimens for getting from point A to point B—no longer spoke to him. Rather, he simply remained open to whatever was arising moment to moment.

Seeing that I was looking for something a bit more tangible, and being a friend of J. Krishnamurti, Burt suggested I follow Krishnamurti's guidelines to meditation:

> [S]it very quietly; do not force yourself to sit quietly, but sit or lie down quietly without force of any kind. . . Then watch your thinking. . . Do not try to change your thinking. . . And when a thought arises, do not condemn it, do not say it is right, it is wrong, it is good, it is bad. Just watch it, so that you begin to have a perception, a consciousness which is active in seeing every kind of thought, every kind of feeling. . . When you look, when you go into thought very very deeply, your mind becomes extraordinarily subtle, alive. No part of the mind is asleep. The mind is completely awake. . . To

understand the whole process of your thinking and feeling is to be free from all thought. . . .[1]

To be free from all thought and feeling isn't to silence
all thought and feeling. On the contrary, trying to silence
thought and feeling only increases your attachment to
thought and feeling. To be free is to simply observe what
is happening. As I sit and observe my mind, I ask myself,
"Who is this observing?" As I watch my mind entertain
thoughts and feelings, I come to realize that the watcher of
this tableau isn't thinking or feeling but merely observing. I
come to realize the spacious mind in which narrow mind of
thoughts and feelings rests, and then, in rare moments, even
this realization ceases and "me" comes to an end. Where I
am not, I'ing is.

PASSAGE MEDITATION

While I never studied with him personally, the teachings
of Eknath Easwaran, a contemporary Indian-born teacher,
author, and spiritual guide, have had a great and beneficial
impact on my life. Passage meditation is one of his great gifts
to humanity. Memorizing a passage of scripture, poetry, or
spiritual teaching for passage meditation is like the planting
a seed of wisdom in the field of "me." Sitting and reciting the
passage in passage meditation is watering the seed. In time
it will sprout and prepare the field of "me" for the greater
sense of I'ing.

You can find passages worthy of memorization in a num-
ber of collections, though I recommend two in particular:
Eknath Easwaran's *God Makes the Rivers to* (Tomales, CA:
Nilgiri Press, 2009) and my own *The World Wisdom Bible*
(Nashville, TN: Skylight Paths, 2017).

Here is a brief description of passage meditation:

Having memorized the passage [of your choosing], be
seated and softly close your eyes. . . [G]o through it word
by word, as slowly as you can. . . The space between
the words is a matter for each person to work out indi-
vidually. They should be comfortably spaced with a
little elbow room between. If the words come too close
together, you will not slow down the mind. . . If the
words stand too far apart, they will not be working
together. . . Concentrate on one word at a time, and let
the words slip one after another into your consciousness,
like pearls falling into a clear pond. . . .[2]

NETI-NETI

Where passage meditation fills a field with wisdom, *Neti-Neti*
plows it all under. Derived from the Hindu Upanishads, *Neti-
Neti* ("Not this. Not this.") speaks to the fact that the God,
wisdom, and reality of your understanding is nothing other
than a product of your imagining and not to be mistaken for
Absolute Reality itself. *Neti-Neti* is "an expression of something inexpressible."[3]

Every time you find yourself ruminating about things—
God, self, nature, the meaning and purpose of life—say to
yourself, "*Neti-Neti*, not this, not this. Nothing I can imagine
is capable of articulating that truth beyond imagining." Whenever you find yourself taking refuge in this or that idea, ism,
or ideology, plow it under by saying to yourself "*Neti-Neti*, not
this, not this." As the psychologist Pavel G. Somov explains,
"When I call upon you to 'neti it out,' I am inviting you to
recognize that *you are not a given this, you are not a given that*."[4]

Neti-Neti leaves you in a mental void. For a moment all
thinking ceases. Everything is just as it is and there is nothing
to say or do about it. You are simply present to the ten thousand joys and ten thousand sorrows of this and every moment.

Neti-Neti is, in a sense, a mental version of Monk Begging for Food: you are simply present without resistance.

THIRD-STEP PRAYER

Here again are the words of the official Third-Step Prayer of AA God:

> I offer myself to Thee—to build with me and to do with me as Thou wilt. Relieve me of the bondage of self, that I may better do Thy will. Take away my difficulties, that victory over them may bear witness to those I would help of Thy Power, Thy Love, and Thy Way of Life. May I do Thy will always![5]

I'm not big on praying. The God of my understanding is reality and asking reality to do anything for me is asking reality to yield to my will. This is self-power on steroids! I'm more comfortable with Anne Lamott who writes, "Don't pray for God to do this or that, or for God's sake to knock it off, or for specific outcomes."[6] Rather yield to spontaneous "prayer" erupting out of your immediate situation without any conscious effort on your part. These lead to the three existential prayers she labels: Help! Thanks! and Wow![7]

When I am crashing to a new rock bottom, I find myself crying out, Help! When I'm gifted with something that serves my flourishing or the flourishing of those I love, I find myself saying, Thanks! And when I'm effortlessly in the stance of Monk Begging for Food and my mind washed clean in the clear water of *Neti-Neti*, I find myself breathlessly mouthing, Wow! I'm not praying to someone or Some One but merely expressing my feelings at that moment. I see the Third-Step Prayer as an expression of all three feelings: Help! Thanks! and Wow! And because I do, I have rewritten the prayer for myself.

Perhaps my version of the prayer will be of value to you, or at the very least it might encourage you to write your own:

> I'm helpless,
> incapable of even offering myself to you,
> so take me, surrender me
> do not wait for me to give permission.
> I'm helpless,
> incapable of imposing my will on anyone, even myself,
> so cleanse me of "me" and make "me" a servant of you.
> Relieve me of the bondage of self,
> And place me in service to truth.
> Don't take away my difficulties,
> just let me not wish them to be taken away.
> Make me a tributary of your power, your love, and your life
> and in this way may I do your will always.

WHO IS THIS ALIVENESS I AM?

In the biblical Book of Nehemiah we find the following teaching, "You alone are God. You made the sky, even the distant heavens and all their stars, the earth and all that dwells upon it, the seas and all that lives within then. You enliven them all" (Nehemiah 9:6). The Hebrew word translated as "enliven" is *m'chayei* from which comes the word *chiut*, the aliveness of all life. Each life is the manifesting of the single process of *chiut*, the aliveness that is God happening in, with, and as each and every happening.

The late eighteenth-century Hasidic sage Menachem Nachum of Chernobyl taught that whenever you have lost the sense of spacious mind and hence the awareness of the I'ing that is God, all you need do is inquire into the *chiut* of "self" and you will awaken as the I'ing of all. My friend and teacher Rabbi David Zeller turned this teaching into a song ("I Am

Alive"). While I can't teach you to sing the song from a book, I can unpack it a bit so that when you do sing it, the invitation of opening to *chiut*/I'ing that is all reality may be accepted.

The song opens with a Hasidic *niggun*, a wordless melody, followed by the affirmation "I am alive":

> Aye lai lai lai lai lai lai lai I am alive
> Aye lai lai lai lai lai lai lai I am alive
> Aye lai lai lai lai lai lai lai I am alive

Think of the *niggun* as the babbling of a baby rejoicing in the sound of her own voice. It is this rejoicing that affirms the fact that you are alive. The "I am" that is alive here is the "me" you imagine yourself to be: the "me" of *mochin d'katnut*, narrow mind; the "me" of *jiriki*, self-power; the "me" that is playing God. This "me" isn't false or demonic. It isn't to be erased, only put in its place: the greater I'ing of *mochin d'gadlu*, spacious mind; the I-ing of *tariki*, other-power; the I'ing that isn't playing God but that is God. You put this lesser "I am" in its proper place by inquiring into the nature of *chiut*, aliveness:

> And who is this aliveness (*chiut*) I am?
> And who is this aliveness (*chiut*) I am?
> And who is this aliveness (*chiut*) I am?

Just asking the question pulls the rug out from under narrow mind's playing God. As you affirm the "me" that is alive, you realize that the one affirming is greater than the one being affirmed. And who is this "greater" I am? Nothing other than reality itself, *Eheyh*, the I'ing happening as all happening, what David Zeller calls the Holy Blessed One:

IS IT NOT THE HOLY BLESSED ONE?

"I Am Alive" is the theme song of my surrendered life, and it pops into my mind regularly. I suggest you listen to David

Zeller sing the song on YouTube, https://www.youtube.com
/watch?v=1npUzSqhtJo, and see if it doesn't do for you what
it does for me: remind "me" of the I'ing I really am.

ENSŌ

An *ensō* (Japanese, "circle") is a hand-drawn circle made with
a single brushstroke. An *ensō* reflects your state of mind.[8]
When drawn from narrow mind, the brushstroke is forced,
inelegant, and hesitant. When drawn from spacious mind, the
brushstroke is effortless, graceful, and bold. Drawing an *ensō*
and then reflecting on the quality of your drawing provides
you with a mirror to your state of mind.

There is no perfect *ensō*, only the *ensō* you draw in the
moment. "The *ensō* ranges in shape from perfectly symmetrical to completely irregular, with brushstrokes either thin and
delicate or broad and massive. . . . [*Ensō*] reflect the artist's
understanding that, at their best, words and images cannot
express the truth completely."[9] Drawing an *ensō* is another
way of getting beyond words and concepts, isms and ideologies, and hence standing naked in the now without the mask
of "me." Figuratively speaking, *ensō* points the God of your
understanding toward the Power Greater than Ourselves.

Many years ago I spent a short time with a Zen teacher (whose name escapes me) practicing *ensō* drawing. As I recall, he taught me to draw the *ensō* quickly and without hesitation or forethought: "Breathe in. Pause. Then breathe out and draw with the out-breath. One circle, one breath. A simple expression of what is." He suggested that I draw a circle each morning and again each evening as a means of peering into my state of mind.

While I have, and you can, purchase special bushes, ink, and paper for your *ensō* drawing, I often draw *ensō* with a Sharpie Pro Magnum Permanent Marker on heavy water-color paper. It isn't as aesthetically pleasing, but it works well enough. I sit at my desk with a blank piece of paper taped or weighted down on the desk surface. (I don't want the paper to shift while I draw.) I hold the brush or Sharpie above the paper, close my eyes, and breathe. When the spirit (breath) moves me, I open my eyes and in one motion draw the *ensō*. I then replace the pen, close my eyes while I breathe a few more times. I then open my eyes to allow first impressions of my drawing to arise. Is the line fluid or jerky? Is the circle solid or broken? I'm not looking for a perfect circle, in fact, I'm less concerned with the roundness of the circle than I am with the line that comprises it. Whatever I find, I place my palms together and bow slightly to my *ensō* to say "Thanks."

You can find YouTube videos for learning how to draw an *ensō*. For example: https://www.youtube.com/watch?v =QLFft9xmnm8))

ACKNOWLEDGMENTS

I wrote this book in a surrendered state. I had no idea how to proceed, and for most of the writing process every sentence seemed shallow and false. I was willfully manipulating thoughts and ideas, and forcing words onto the screen. My body reacted negatively as well. I was plagued by blinding migraines that prevented me from working, and uncontrollable tremors that kept my fingers typing long past the point of making sense. And I slept sometimes twenty hours a day. I don't imagine this book caused any of this, but it grew out of it.

Physically and emotionally exhausted, I was forced to abandon the task and put the project on hold for months. Without making a decision to do so—and contrary to everything that is true about me and how I work—I let the whole thing drop. Until I didn't.

I awoke one morning around 3:30 and I simply knew what to say. Of course, what arises at such early morning moments of clarity isn't a fully formed book. There is a craft to writing: you hone the raw words into sentences and paragraphs and chapters that are compelling and meaningful and worthy of the reader's time and energy. I have honed this craft in over thirty books over the course of half a century, but I never mastered it. That's why I am so very grateful to work with Emily Wichland, my editor at Turner Publishing. Emily and I have collaborated on over a dozen books, and each time we do so I am amazed at her skill at improving my writing and sharpening my thinking. So, Emily, thank you once again.

Before sending the book to Emily I sent it to my friends and colleagues Frank Levy, director of the One River Foundation, and Gordon Peerman, an Episcopal priest, Buddhist meditation teacher, and author of *Blessed Relief: What Christians Can Learn from Buddhists about Suffering*, a book he too wrote with Emily's help. Gordon and Frank, thanks for making time to help me with this.

When Emily returned the edited manuscript to me I was once again in the grips of migraines, tremors, and now sleep deprivation that made writing very difficult for me. I turned to my son Aaron, a poet, author, and professor of English, for help. He patiently explained what needed to be done with this book. After a few weeks, and with his help, I have done my best to do it. Thanks, Boy.

This book is also enriched by the wisdom and struggles of numerous women and men in Twelve Step programs. I am grateful to each of them for sharing their insights with me, and, by extension, with you.

I am especially grateful to Burt, my first and forever sponsor, whose guidance informs every page of this book. While his life has ended (Burt died during the writing of this book) his wisdom is timeless. Thank you, Brother, for everything.

While in no way endorsed by AA World Services, my use of the Twelve Steps is done with their permission. I have adapted the language of the Twelve Steps to be more inclusive regarding both gender and addiction. My understanding and interpretation of the Steps is, of course, mine alone.

Given my health and its impact on my ability to write, I suspect this to be my final book. I could be wrong; I often am, but in any case thank you for talking this journey with me.

NOTES

PREFACE

1. Hiroyuki Itsuki, *Tariki: Embracing Despair, Discovering Peace* (New York: Kodansha America, 2001), 129.

LIVING THE SURRENDERED LIFE, A PREVIEW

1. Inspired by the teachings of Pema Chodron.

INTRODUCTION

1. *Alcoholics Anonymous: The Big Book*, 4th Edition (New York: Alcoholics Anonymous, Inc., 2006), 30.
2. *Alcoholics Anonymous: The Big Book*, 4th Edition (New York: Alcoholics Anonymous, Inc., 2006), 30.
3. *Alcoholics Anonymous: The Big Book*, 4th Edition (New York: Alcoholics Anonymous, Inc., 2006), 62.
4. *Twelve Steps and Twelve Traditions* (New York: Alcoholics Anonymous, Inc., 2004), 21.

CHAPTER 1: YOU ARE THE PROBLEM

1. Walpola Rahula, *What the Buddha Taught* (New York: Grove Press, 1974), 61.
2. Rami Shapiro, *Ecclesiastes: Annotated & Explained* (Woodstock, VT: SkyLight Paths, 2010), 27–29.
3. Joseph Campbell, in Gabor Maté, *In the Realm of Hungry Ghosts: Close Encounters with Addiction* (Berkeley, CA: North Atlantic Books, 2010), 418.

CHAPTER 2: I GOTTA BE ME

1. Richard Hughes, *A High Wind in Jamaica* (Boston: Harper, 1929), 135–137.
2. Richard Hughes, *A High Wind in Jamaica* (Boston: Harper, 1929), 138.

3. Albert Einstein, cited in Alice Calaprice, ed., *The New Quotable Einstein* (Princeton, NJ: Princeton University Press, 2005), 206.

CHAPTER 3: STOP ME'ING

1. Erich Fromm, *To Have or To Be?* New York: Harper & Row, 1976), 24.

2. Erich Fromm, *To Have or To Be?* (New York: Harper & Row, 1976), 27; italics in the original.

3. J. Krishnamurti. *Choiceless Awareness* (Ojai, CA: Krishnamurti Foundation of American, 1992), 7.

CHAPTER 4: THE TAO OF YOU

1. David Gregson and Jay Efran. *The Tao of Sobriety* (New York: St. Martin's Press, 2002), 1.

2. David Hinton, *Existence: A Story* (Boulder, CO: Shambhala, 2016), 36.

3. David Hinton, *Existence: A Story* (Boston, MA: Shambhala, 2016), 14.

4. Alan Watts, *The Wisdom of Insecurity* (New York: Vintage, 2011), 32.

5. Aaron James, *Surfing with Sartre: An Aquatic Inquiry into a Life of Meaning* (New York: Doubleday, 2017), 27.

6. Thich Nhat Hahn, *Zen Keys: A Guide to Zen Practice* (New York: Harmony, 1994), 42, adapted.

7. Alan Watts, *What Is Tao?* (Novato, CA: New World Library, 2000), 50.

8. Alan Watts, *What Is Tao?* (Novato, CA: New World Library, 2000), 61–62.

CHAPTER 5: BEING POWERLESS

1. Thomas Keating, *Divine Therapy & Addiction: Centering Prayer and the Twelves Steps* (New York: Lantern Books, 2009), 9.

2. Thomas Keating, *Divine Therapy & Addiction: Centering Prayer and the Twelves Steps* (New York: Lantern Books, 2009), 11.

3. Judith Orloff, *The Ecstasy of Surrender* (New York: Harmony Books, 2014), xv.

4. Judith Orloff, *The Ecstasy of Surrender* (New York: Harmony Books, 2014), 386.

5. *Alcoholics Anonymous: The Big Book*, 4th Edition (New York: Alcoholics Anonymous, Inc., 2006), 63.

6. J. Krishnamurti, *Choiceless Awareness* (Ojai, CA: Krishnamurti Foundation of America, 2001), 77; italics in the original.

7. Thomas Keating, *Divine Therapy & Addiction: Centering Prayer and the Twelves Steps* (New York: Lantern Books, 2009), 26–27.

CHAPTER 6: YES, AND

1. Bob Kulhan and Chuck Crisafulli, *Getting to "Yes, And": The Art of Business Improvisation* (Stanford, CA: Stanford University Press, 2017), 27.

CHAPTER 7: ROCK BOTTOM

1. Susan Anderson, *The Journey from Abandonment to Healing* (New York: Penguin, 2000), 15.

CHAPTER 8: CAME TO BELIEVE

1. Noson Yanofsky, *The Outer Limits of Reason* (Cambridge, MA: Massachusetts Institute of Technology, 2013), 2.

2. Andrew Newberg, *Why God Won't Go Away: Brain Science and the Biology of Belief* (New York: Random House, 2001), 152.

3. Albert Einstein, *Einstein on Cosmic Religion and Other Opinions & Aphorisms* (New York: Covici-Friede, 1931), 48–49.

CHAPTER 9: A POWER GREATER THAN OURSELVES

1. *Alcoholics Anonymous: The Big Book*, 4th Edition (New York: Alcoholics Anonymous, Inc., 2006), 13.

2. *Alcoholics Anonymous: The Big Book*, 4th Edition (New York: Alcoholics Anonymous, Inc., 2006), 14, 24.

3. *Alcoholics Anonymous: The Big Book*, 4th Edition (New York: Alcoholics Anonymous, Inc., 2006), 24.

4. *Alcoholics Anonymous: The Big Book*, 4th Edition (New York: Alcoholics Anonymous, Inc., 2006), 24.

5. *Alcoholics Anonymous: The Big Book*, 4th Edition (New York: Alcoholics Anonymous, Inc., 2006), 60.

6. *Alcoholics Anonymous: The Big Book*, 4th Edition (New York: Alcoholics Anonymous, Inc., 2006), 62.

7. *Alcoholics Anonymous: The Big Book*, 4th Edition. New York: Alcoholics Anonymous, Inc., 2006), 45; italics in the original.

8. *Alcoholics Anonymous: The Big Book*, 4th Edition (New York: Alcoholics Anonymous, Inc., 2006), 47.

9. *Alcoholics Anonymous: The Big Book*, 4th Edition (New York: Alcoholics Anonymous, Inc., 2006), 55.

Chapter 10: Glimpsing the Unglimpsable

1. Alan Watts, *The Meaning of Happiness* (New York: Harper Colophon, 1979), 119–120.

Chapter 11: Purpose

1. Rick Warren, *The Purpose Driven Life* (Grand Rapids: Zondervan, 2002), 23.

2. Rick Warren, *The Purpose Driven Life* (Grand Rapids: Zondervan, 2002), 24–25.

3. J. Krishnamurti, *On Love and Loneliness* (New York: HarperCollins Publishers, 1993), 45.

Chapter 12: Beyond Happiness

1. Aristotle, *Nicomachean Ethics*, book 1, chapt. 7.5, trans. Terence Irwin (Indianapolis: Hackett, 1999), 8.

2. Dalai Lama, *The Art of Happiness* (New York: Riverhead Books, 1998), 13.

3. Dalai Lama, *The Art of Happiness* (New York: Riverhead Books, 1998), 15.

4. Dalai Lama, *The Art of Happiness* (New York: Riverhead Books, 1998), 24; italics in the original.

5. Dalai Lama, *The Art of Happiness* (New York: Riverhead Books, 1998), 26.

6. Alan Watts, *The Meaning of Happiness* (New York: Harper Colophon, 1979), 147.

Chapter 13: God as We Understood God

1. *Alcoholics Anonymous: The Big Book*, 4th Edition (New York: Alcoholics Anonymous, Inc., 2006), 12.

2. *Alcoholics Anonymous: The Big Book*, 4th Edition. New York: Alcoholics Anonymous, Inc., 2006, p. 12, italics in the original.

3. *Twelve Steps and Twelve Traditions* (New York: Alcoholics Anonymous, Inc., 2002), 34.

4. *Alcoholics Anonymous: The Big Book*, 4th Edition (New York: Alcoholics Anonymous, Inc., 2006), 13.

5. *Twelve Steps and Twelve Traditions* (New York: Alcoholics Anonymous, Inc., 2002), 27.

6. *Twelve Steps and Twelve Traditions* (New York: Alcoholics Anonymous, Inc., 2002), 103–104; italics in the original.

7. *Alcoholics Anonymous: The Big Book*, 4th Edition (New York: Alcoholics Anonymous, Inc., 2006), 46–47.

CHAPTER 14: THE ETERNAL TAO

1. *Alcoholics Anonymous: The Big Book*, 4th Edition (New York: Alcoholics Anonymous, Inc., 2006), 63, italics in the original.

2. *Alcoholics Anonymous: The Big Book*, 4th Edition (New York: Alcoholics Anonymous, Inc., 2006), 63, italics in the original.

3. Jonah Goldberg, *Suicide of the West*. (New York: Crown Forum, 2018), 5.

4. Alan Watts, *The Meaning of Happiness* (New York: Harper Colophon, 1979), 179.

5. Alan Watts, *The Meaning of Happiness* (New York: Harper Colophon, 1979), 180.

CHAPTER 15: YOUR WILL, YOUR LIFE

1. Thich Nhat Hanh, *The Heart of Understanding: Commentaries on the Prajnaparamita Heart Sutra*. (Berkeley: Parallax Press, 1998), 3.

2. Alan Watts, *The Book: On the Taboo Against Knowing Who You Are*. (New York: Vintage, 1989), 94.

CHAPTER 16: BEING NOBODY

1. Albert Einstein, in a letter written in 1950, quoted in the *New York Times*, March 29, 1972.

2. Martin Buber, *I and Thou*, trans. Ronald Gregor Smith (New York: Charles Scribner's Sons, 1986), 19.

3. Martin Buber, *The Way of Man according to the Teaching of Hasidism* (Secaucus, NJ: Citadel Press, 1994), 12–13, adapted.

CHAPTER 17: GOD'S CARE, GOD'S GRACE

1. Rami Shapiro, *Amazing Chesed: Living a Grace-Filled Judaism* (Woodstock, VT: Jewish Lights Publishing, 2013), 8.
2. Alan Watts, *The Meaning of Happiness* (New York: Harper Colophon, 1979), 132.
3. Taitetsu Unno, *River of Fire, River of Water* (New York: Doubleday, 1998), 123.
4. Ichitaro, quoted in Taitetsu Unno, *River of Fire, River of Water* (New York: Doubleday, 1998), 123.

CHAPTER 18: LETTING GO OF DECIDING

1. Katie Goodman, *Improvisation for the Spirit*. (Naperville, IL: Sourcebooks, 2008), 99.

CHAPTER 19: LIVING SURRENDERED

1. Alan Watts, *The Book: On the Taboo Against Knowing Who You Are* (New York: Vintage, 1989), 84.
2. Alan Watts, *The Meaning of Happiness* (New York: Harper Colophon, 1979), 184.
3. Aaron James, *Surfing with Sartre: An Aquatic Inquiry into a Life of Meaning* (New York: Doubleday, 2017), 49–51.

CHAPTER 20: SERENITY

1. Shantideva, *The Way of the Bodhisattva*, trans. Padmakare Translation Group (Boston: Shambhala, 2006), 79, adapted.

CHAPTER 21: FREEDOM OF IMPERFECTION

1. John Louis Cimasi, *Vignettes from a Life: Living Wabi Sabi* (North Charleston, SC: CreateSpace, 2015), xxix.
2. Julie Pointer Adams, *Wabi-Sabi Welcome* (New York: Artisan, 2017), 18.
3. Leonard Koren, *Wabi–Sabi for Artists, Designers, Poets & Philosophers* (Berkeley: Stone Bridge Press, 1994), 40.

4. Marie Kondo, *The Life-Changing Magic of Tidying Up: The Japanese Art of Decluttering and Organizing* (Berkeley: Ten Speed Press, 2014), 41.

5. Andrew Juniper, *Wabi-Sabi: The Japanese Art of Impermanence* (Rutland, VT: Tuttle Publishing, 2003), 105.

CHAPTER 22: INNER SEEING

1. Gregg Krech, *Naikan: Gratitude, Grace and the Japanese Art of Self–Reflection* (Berkeley, CA: Stone Bridge Press, 2002), 26.

2. Gregg Krech, *Naikan: Gratitude, Grace and the Japanese Art of Self–Reflection* (Berkeley, CA: Stone Bridge Press, 2002), 29.

3. "Group to Combat Alcoholism Grows Apace in Anonymity," *Christian Science Monitor*, January 8, 1944, p. 3.

4. Ralph Waldo Emerson, "Compensation," in *The Essential Writings of Ralph Waldo Emerson* (New York: Random House, 2000), 164.

5. Gregg Krech, *Naikan: Gratitude, Grace and the Japanese Art of Self–Reflection* (Berkeley, CA: Stone Bridge Press, 2002), 57.

6. Henry David Thoreau, *Walden* (Macon, GA: Mercer University Press, 2011), 88.

CHAPTER 23: FORGIVENESS

1. Rhonda Byrne, *The Secret* (Hillsboro, OR: Beyond Words Publishing, 2006), 7.

2. Rhonda Byrne, *The Secret* (Hillsboro, OR: Beyond Words Publishing, 2006), 30.

CHAPTER 24: HUMILITY

1. *Twelve Steps and Twelve Traditions* (New York: Alcoholics Anonymous, Inc., 2002), 70.

2. Hubert Benoit, *Zen and the Psychology of Transformation: The Supreme Doctrine* (Rochester, VT: Inner Traditions International, 1990), 237).

3. Hubert Benoit, *Zen and the Psychology of Transformation: The Supreme Doctrine* (Rochester, VT: Inner Traditions International, 1990), 239.

INVITATIONS

1. J. Krishnamurti, *On Education* (London: Krishnamurti Foundation Trust Ltd., 1974), 58.

2. Eknath Easwaran, *Passage Meditation* (Tomales, CA: Nilgiri Press, 2016), 4–6.

3. L. C. Beckett, *Neti-Neti: Not This, Not That* (London: John M. Watkins, 1959), 29.

4. Pavel G. Somov, *The Lotus Effect: Shedding Suffering and Rediscovering Your Essential Self* (Oakland, CA: New Harbinger Publications, 2010), 34, italics in the original.

5. *Alcoholics Anonymous: The Big Book*, 4th Edition (New York: Alcoholics Anonymous, Inc., 2006), 63.

6. Anne Lamott, *Help, Thanks, Wow: The Three Essential Prayers* (New York: Penguin Group, 2012), 15.

7. Lamott, *Help, Thanks, Wow.*

8. Audrey Yoshiko Seo, *Ensō: Zen Circles of Enlightenment* (Boston: Weatherhill, 2007, xii).

9. Audrey Yoshiko Seo, *Ensō: Zen Circles of Enlightenment* (Boston: Weatherhill, 2007, xii).

SUGGESTIONS FOR FURTHER READING

Alexander, William. *Cool Water: Alcoholism, Mindfulness, and Ordinary Recovery*. Boston: Shambhala, 1997.

Chodron, Pema. *When Things Fall Apart*. Boston: Shambhala, 2016.

Dalai Lama. *How to See Yourself as You Really Are*. New York: Atria Books, 2006.

Katie, Byron. *Loving What Is: Four Questions That Can Change Your Life*. New York: Harmony Books, 2002.

Lao Tzu, *Tao Te Ching: Annotated & Explained*, Derek Lin (author, translator). Nashville: SkyLight Paths, 2006.

Maharshi, Ramana. *Talks with Ramana Maharshi*. San Diego: Inner Directions, 2000.

May, Gerald. *Addiction and Grace*. New York: HarperCollins Publishers, 1991.

Pitman, Bill. *AA: The Way It Began*. Seattle: Glen Abbey Books, 1988.

Reynolds, David. *Constructive Living*. Honolulu: University of Hawaii Press, 1984.

Reynolds, David. *A Handbook for Constructive Living*. Honolulu: University of Hawaii Press, 2002.

Shapiro, Rami. Recovery—The Sacred Art: The Twelve Steps as Spiritual Practice. Woodstock, VT: SkyLight Paths, 2009.

———. *Perennial Wisdom for the Spiritually Independent, Sacred Teachings Annotated & Explained*. Woodstock, VT: SkyLight Paths, 2013.

———. *The Sacred Art of Lovingkindness*. Nashville: SkyLight Paths, 2006.

———. *The World Wisdom Bible: A New Testament for a Global Spirituality*. Nashville: SkyLight Paths, 2016.

Unno, Taitetsu. *Shin Buddhism, Bits of Rubble Turn into Gold*. New York: Doubleday, 2002.

Watts, Alan. *Tao: Watercourse Way*. New York: Pantheon Books, 1975.

ABOUT THE AUTHOR

A Jewish practitioner of Perennial Wisdom, Rabbi Rami Shapiro is an award-winning author of over thirty books on religion and spirituality. He received rabbinical ordination from the Hebrew Union College–Jewish Institute of Religion, and holds a PhD in religion from Union Graduate School. A chaplain with the USAF for three years, a congregational rabbi for twenty, and a professor of religious studies for ten, Rabbi Rami currently helps direct the One River Foundation (www.oneriverfoundation.org), writes the "Roadside Assistance for the Spiritual Traveler" column for *Spirituality and Health* magazine, and hosts the magazine's weekly podcast, "Essential Conversations with Rabbi Rami." His first book on Twelve-Step spirituality was *Recovery: The Sacred Art*. His newest book is *The World Wisdom Bible* (Turner Publishing, 2017).

Printed in the USA
CPSIA information can be obtained
at www.ICGtesting.com
JSHW022322140824
68134JS00019B/1233